WHOLE BOWLS

WHOLE BOWLS

**Complete Gluten-Free and Vegetarian
Meals to Power Your Day**

Allison Day

Skyhorse Publishing
New York

Skyhorse Publishing books may be purchased in bulk at special discounts for sales promotion, corporate gifts, fund-raising, or educational purposes. Special editions can also be created to specifications. For details, contact the Special Sales Department, Skyhorse Publishing, 307 West 36th Street, 11th Floor, New York, NY 10018 or info@skyhorsepublishing.com.

Skyhorse® and Skyhorse Publishing® are registered trademarks of Skyhorse Publishing, Inc.®, a Delaware corporation.

Visit our website at www.skyhorsepublishing.com.

10 9 8 7 6 5 4 3

Library of Congress Cataloging-in-Publication Data is available on file.

Cover design by Laura Klynstra
Cover photo credit Allison Day

Print ISBN: 978-1-63450-855-1
Ebook ISBN: 978-1-63450-856-8

Printed in the United States of America

For my Dad.

CONTENTS

Introduction

One good bowl will take you far.

I grabbed a spoon and cozied up on the couch with a blanket, a book on my lap, and a dog at my feet. Comforting, warm, and greedily proportioned, I tucked into my bowl of dinner with abandon. Beads of brown rice, golden coins of sweet potato, a grassy mountain of steamed kale, and a scoop of chickpeas. The sauce was the anchor, keeping everything grounded—simply tamari, olive oil, and balsamic vinegar drizzled on every component until it looked right to me (no measurement). This recipe wasn't special or sophisticated or something I wrote down to share, but it was all I needed and then some. My meal comprised the previous night's leftovers and a batch of chickpeas I had cooked and frozen, assembled on the fly when hunger pangs set in that evening. It made me feel full and happy and taken care of. I could choose my bites with precision, cherry-picking a morsel of each element with every spoonful.

The bowl itself was something I'd use as inspiration for dinner the next day; maybe I'd fill it with pasta—but not before breakfast in the morning with oatmeal, a tumble of blueberries, and walnuts as decoration. A large salad with greens and grains and beans for lunch would sit pretty within the curved walls. And for dessert, ice cream perhaps, or rice pudding.

It was this one bowl, a rather ugly one—faded white, oddly shaped, with fork scratches on the bottom and a chip on its shoulder—that would inspire many more plentiful meals to come. This one ugly duckling bowl full of this and that from the refrigerator and pantry, composed neatly, eaten messily, and nearly licked clean (then literally licked clean when no one was watching), helped me come up with the concept for a series of dishes for my recipe blog, *Yummy Beet*, followed by this very book.

For *Whole Bowls*, my goal was to create an entire cookbook of these much-loved, visually alluring, mouthwatering, and aromatic recipes that would find themselves at home within the walls of this snug serving vessel any time of day. None of the ingredients would stand alone, working harmoniously for a healthy meal concept that focused on abundance, not restriction. These recipes, like the ones I create for *Yummy Beet*, are a tribute to fresh, local, seasonal foods, and the vibrant international flavors that I find so appealing. They're wholesome, plant-based, balanced, one-bowl meals that not only taste delicious, but ignite every other sense simultaneously.

Whole Bowls is about flexibility. Make a little today. Save a few key components for a week of packable lunches. Mix and match the ingredients. Freeze a batch of grains and beans. Use this sauce over that sauce. These bowls are ideal for solo cooks as much as they are for an entire family, with the ability to be transformed into an elegant meal for guests or yourself, or eaten casually standing at the counter late into the night.

Quite simply, there is no precept to these dishes, including how you eat them, serve them, and savor them. Some may want to enjoy each component separately, like a well-organized painter's palette, jumping into a different element with each bite, while others may feel compelled to mix it all together. For my perfect bite, a little bit of everything needs to hop onto my utensil: crunchy, creamy, acidic, salty, sweet, and bitter.

Whatever your method of operation, the recipes you'll find in these pages emphasize accessibility, everyday luxury, and pleasure.

In brief, *Whole Bowls* is a guide to practical vegetable, grain, protein, and condiment (and dessert) recipes that all come together with my straightforward build-a-bowl approach—a theory you can try for yourself with **The Whole Bowls Formula**.

The formula is simple, and best of all, versatile. This is not only with regards to the ingredients, but the number of diners who can enjoy these complete, meal-in-a-bowl feasts. Many of the grains, protein options, condiments, and vegetables that are integral to the formula can be made ahead, pared down, or traded for another component in an entirely different recipe. The choice is yours; these recipes are meant to be unfussed, unhurried, and rule-free.

Though this cookbook is fully vegetarian with many wholly vegan options and plant-based substitutions, it's by all means meant for every dietary preference, containing a range of familiar flavors that will appeal to even the most steadfast meat-eater. I like to think of the recipes as a jumping-off point; a blueprint for consuming more vegetables, fruits, whole grains, beans, and legumes, whether that be at every meal of the day or one plant-packed meal per week. The recipes and ingredients in this book are not to be "alternatives" in the dietary fringe sense, being enticing, exciting, and delicious as-is.

In addition to being vegetarian, the recipes you'll find in here are gluten-free—naturally so—a way I've been cooking almost exclusively for a decade following my sister's celiac disease diagnosis. Though brown rice, quinoa, buckwheat, and all other inherently gluten-free whole grains need no validation of their versatility and exquisite flavor, in the name of flexibility, if a gluten-containing grain or pasta is more to your liking, feel free to replace the gluten-free option I've laid out in the recipes. Whole grain, gluten-containing trades I enjoy include spelt (especially the pasta), barley, wheat berries, and rye.

And, while I won't tell you what to eat, I did have a few requirements for the bowls in this book. First, accessibility to every skill level and kitchen size. Second, I wanted complete meal bowls for all dining opportunities, including dessert for those with a sweet tooth (me). Third, the recipes had to be balanced, not just nutritionally (as a nutritionist, I do think about these things), but also flavor-, color-, and texture-wise. Each component really does need to be seasoned generously, not only with salt, but also spices, acids, colors, and textures—bowls are truly multisensory. Finally, each bowl had to be lip-smacking and feel a touch luxurious

because I love to eat tasty, beautiful food, no matter the label attached.

Enjoying a meal from a bowl is a ritual all ages, countries, and cuisines can and do take part in. It's cold cereal. It's soup. It's salad. It's porridge. It's pasta. It's all for you or served family-style for all. Bowls allow us to sit, relish, and stop, if only for a moment, which, in my opinion, is a large part of the reason so many choose them when reaching into the cupboard.

It's time to get excited about plant- and vegetable-focused cooking and eating.

Whether a bowl contains bold, in-your-face flavors, or is muted and mild, there's something in here to suit every taste, diner, time constraint, and desire. Follow the recipes to a "T." Reincarnate last night's dinner for tomorrow's lunch. Whip up a few staples and basics. Treat yourself. Entertain your friends (or yourself) with something unexpected. Let your imagination go wild. It's time to celebrate imaginative, plentiful, plant-based, meal-in-a-bowl dishes that do a body, the planet, and most importantly, your taste buds, a world of good.

Vegetarian Pantry Guide

I can't live without a well-stocked pantry (I'm much like a Hobbit this way), which is why I've devoted an entire chapter to my ingredient essentials. Many of the items are used several times throughout this cookbook, so don't be hesitant about going a little overboard when buying items in bulk. From oils to mustards, almonds to seaweed sprinkles, keeping the following pantry items at arm's reach enables you to construct delicious, healthy, home-cooked meals any day of the week. If you're just starting to prepare more whole foods at home, please don't become overwhelmed by this chapter—begin slowly, building your pantry with one or two new items a week, and you'll be fully stocked before you know it.

OILS AND FATS

Butter: Butter's flavor is unmatched. Like eggs and dairy, I do my best to seek out organic butter for animal well-being reasons, which is readily available in most supermarkets today.

Coconut oil: The virgin variety has a mellow tropical aroma, buttery taste, and silky texture. For those who aren't keen on the taste, refined coconut oil is free of any coconut flavor.

Extra-virgin olive oil: Ideal for dressing, drizzling, sautéing, and roasting, no pantry is complete without extra-virgin olive oil. Go for quality here—you'll truly notice the difference, especially when employing the oil as a salad dressing base.

Flaxseed oil: One of the richest sources of plant-based omega-3 fatty acids, holding an exquisite nutty taste and striking, eponymously flaxen hue. Be sure to never heat flaxseed oil, as the healthy fats will turn rancid. Use as a salad dressing, drizzle on warm grains (brown rice, quinoa, oatmeal), steamed vegetables, and more.

Refined avocado oil: Excellent for very high temperature cooking up to 500°F. Neutral in taste, it lends itself well to Asian-inspired dressings, baked goods, and homemade mayonnaise.

Specialty oils: Rich, toasted sesame oil, evergreen-hued roasted pumpkin seed oil, and sweet and nutty hazelnut oil are among my most used. These are to be used judiciously, as the taste can overpower a dish.

GLUTEN-FREE WHOLE GRAINS

Amaranth: These diminutive grains contain a fair amount of iron and plant-based protein. Amaranth can be cooked into porridge, stirred into soups to thicken, and purchased as flour (or made at home in a blender) for gluten-free baked goods. I use it exclusively for porridges, risottos, or puddings, capitalizing on its inherent creaminess.

Black rice: Sometimes called forbidden rice, this inky whole grain is one of the richest sources of antioxidants among any food (grain or otherwise). The flavor is similar to short grain brown rice, yet slightly sweeter, and it's just as easy to prepare, only looking tuxedo-required.

Brown rice: Chewy, dense, and loaded with nutty flavor, brown rice is in heavy rotation in my kitchen. I favor the short grain variety; however, brown basmati rice is a gorgeously scented and light alternative that I utilize as a bed for curries.

Buckwheat and kasha: Contrary to its name, buckwheat doesn't contain any wheat or gluten. Buckwheat groats are a fine alternative to oats for breakfast, even working well uncooked, soaked overnight for a muesli-type dish. Kasha is the toasted version of buckwheat groats, common in Eastern European cooking, and ideal for savory use with its heady aroma and molasses taste.

Millet: Delivering an abundance of minerals, millet is my go-to whole grain and gluten-free replacement for couscous (a small wheat pasta). While it has the ability to be light and fluffy, it can also be blended into mashed potatoes for an ultra-creamy side dish or turned into "polenta" in lieu of cornmeal.

Oats (rolled, steel cut, oat groats, and oat flour): Keeping a cupboard full of oats means that a healthy breakfast is within reach any day of the week. Large flake rolled oats make a delightfully crisp granola, steel cut and oat groats create a hearty base for porridge or risotto, and oat flour can be employed in baking.

A note for those with celiac disease: Oats can trigger a similar immune response as wheat, so incorporate sparingly into your diet and always purchase certified gluten-free and/or wheat-free.

Teff: The smallest grain in the world with a slight nutty flavor and an enviable nutritional profile. Containing calcium, iron, and fiber, it can be made into a creamy cereal, (cooked) chilled and pan-fried in wedges, as well as added to veggie burgers, baked goods, pancakes, and the like for a pleasing textural boost. While still uncommon in the everyday kitchen, it's a grain worth giving a spin.

Quinoa: The original fast food, this protein-packed grain cooks up in less than 20 minutes. Light yet substantial, quinoa's versatility makes it ideal for anytime of day, be that a warm cereal, a cold salad, or sweet dessert.

BEANS AND LEGUMES

1 (15-ounce) can beans = 1½ cups cooked

Black beans: One of the highest protein beans. You may see them labeled as black turtle beans, but they're the same thing. I use these in soups, stews, chili, enchiladas, burritos, and bean dips.

Butter beans: Large, flat, creamy, and fun to eat and say, butter beans feel at home in both everyday and special occasion dishes.

Chickpeas/garbanzo beans: Known best for its role in hummus, you'll see chickpeas used in a host of ways throughout these pages. Canned are great; however, like all of my beans and legumes, I usually cook my own (I do so in a pressure cooker) as the texture, taste, and price tag are much better.

Lentils: Lentils cook up in about 30 minutes and don't require pre-soaking, making these little gems ideal for the time-crunched cook. They come in many varieties, most being interchangeable with the exception of red lentils, which cook down to a thick mash. Because lentils cook so quickly, I recommend cooking them from dry, as opposed to working with canned lentils, which are mushy and, frankly, unappetizing.

Specialty and heirloom beans: For something a little more exciting, specialty and heirloom beans are as delicious as they are beautiful. For sourcing specialty and heirloom beans, California-based Rancho Gordo has you covered with their impressive selection of hand-painted-looking beans (http://ranchogordo.com/).

White beans: The creamiest of the bean family, white beans (sometimes called cannellini beans), are ideal for soups, stews, crostini toppings, and purées. They absorb flavor well, giving you the perfect opportunity to use the more assertive spices and herbs in your kitchen.

TOFU AND SOY PRODUCTS

Edamame: You've likely seen edamame at Japanese restaurants. These emerald pods are packed with protein. Edamame makes an ideal addition to a salad, slaw, or stir-fry. Find shelled edamame in the freezer section of the supermarket.

Tofu (extra-firm, extra-firm silken, and smoked): I choose an extra-firm variety (including extra-firm silken) as I enjoy the hearty texture and ability to be stewed, pan-fried, grilled, baked, and blended (in the case of the extra-firm silken variety). In a few recipes, I call for smoked tofu, now readily available in most supermarkets. If you can't find smoked tofu, a sprinkle of smoked paprika to finish off the dish will provide a similar flavor.

Tempeh: Nutty and dense with a subdued acidic flavor, tempeh is simply fermented soybeans packed into a cake. I enjoy crumbling this into chili and Bolognese sauces for that trademark "meaty" texture (without any of that fake veg-meat). Like tofu, it picks up flavors beautifully, lending itself well to marinades and sauces.

VINEGARS AND ACIDS

Apple cider vinegar: I use unpasteurized (raw) apple cider vinegar with "mother," however, pasteurized apple cider vinegar is interchangeable. The flavor is sharp, perking up any dish you add it to.

Balsamic vinegar: Sweet, almost syrupy, balsamic vinegar heightens a variety of dishes. I often use this in salad dressings, but it can work equally well drizzled over berries and vanilla ice cream.

Rice vinegar (unseasoned): Muted, tangy, and bright, I think of this as the lemon of the vinegar world. While this appears mostly in the Asian-inspired dishes in this cookbook, it can be used in place of distilled white and white wine vinegars as a softer alternative.

Citrus (fresh and bottled lemon, lime, and orange juices): If something tastes a tad bland, a squeeze of fresh lemon juice nearly always solves the problem. Lime juice has a floral aroma to its peel and flesh, marrying beautifully with Thai and Mexican flavors. And orange juice can be used as a natural sweetener in granolas, desserts, dressings, and even roasted vegetables (it's especially nice with beets).

SALT, SPICES, AND DRIED HERBS

The ingredients listed below are the most-used in my recipes, but are certainly not exclusive—add or subtract the ones you enjoy. I purchase salt, spices, and dried herbs at bulk food stores (or in the bulk section of the supermarket) for greater variety—it's also much more economical.

- **Black peppercorns (grind fresh for best flavor)**
- **Chili flakes (sometimes called red pepper flakes)**
- **Cinnamon**
- **Cumin**
- **Curry powder (mild or hot)**
- **Garam masala**
- **Nutmeg**
- **Rosemary (whole)**
- **Saffron**
- **Sea salt (fine-grain)**
- **Smoked paprika**
- **Thyme (whole)**

SEA VEGETABLES

Agar agar: Looking a lot like ice shavings, this clear seaweed is the vegetarian alternative to gelatin. It sets liquids, making it excellent for desserts. Agar agar is flavorless (meaning your dessert won't taste like the sea, if this was concerning you).

Dulse or kelp granules and powder: I refer to these as seaweed sprinkles. Rich in iodine, iron, and an array of other health-promoting minerals, seaweed granules are a superb addition to any recipe.

Nori: If you've eaten sushi, you're probably familiar with nori (it's the evergreen wrapper they use to encase the rice). Nori has a pleasant flavor that pairs particularly well with tamari.

BEVERAGES, CONDIMENTS, AND CANNED GOODS

- **Almond milk, tetra (or boxed) packs (unsweetened, plain)**
- **Coconut milk, canned (full-fat)**
- **Dijon mustard and whole grain mustard**
- **Miso (white shiro miso, red aka miso, yellow shinshu miso, soy-free chickpea miso, and soy-free brown rice miso)**
- **Nutritional yeast (not to be confused with brewer's yeast)**
- **Soy milk, tetra (or boxed) packs (unsweetened, plain)**
- **Tamari (gluten-free)**
- **Tomatoes, canned (whole and paste)**
- **Worcestershire sauce (gluten-free, vegan)**

NUTS AND SEEDS

Almonds: High in vitamin E, fiber, and protein, almonds are the original healthy snack. Store raw almonds in the refrigerator or freezer to keep their delicate oils from expiring too quickly.

Cashews: Raw cashews, when soaked in water and blended, become a dairy-free cream for use in both sweet and savory recipes. Raw or roasted, they can add a pleasing crunch to stir-fries and salads. Store raw cashews in the refrigerator or freezer to keep their delicate oils from expiring too quickly.

Chia seeds: Chia seeds are a wonderful egg replacement in baking, instant-pudding maker, and nutrient-enhancer that can be added to just about any recipe thanks to their neutral taste. High in iron, calcium, and fiber, chia seeds are a low-allergen way to get the health benefits of the nut and seed world into your daily routine. Store chia seeds in the pantry or refrigerator.

Coconut flakes or shredded coconut (dried, unsweetened): Technically a fruit, but used in a similar fashion as nuts and seeds. Aromatic, naturally sweet, and versatile. Add to granola before baking, toss with quinoa, throw in cookie dough, stir into curries, blend to make shelf-stable coconut butter, or eat out of hand. Store coconut flakes or shredded coconut in the pantry.

Nut butters: Seek out natural nut butters (peanut butter, almond butter, etc.) without added oil, salt, or sugar. A little trick for easy mixing that works for all nut and seed butters: keep unopened jars in the pantry upside-down, then give them a vigorous stir to blend before storing in the refrigerator.

Pumpkin, sunflower, and hemp seeds: A lower-allergen alternative to nuts, these everyday seeds are a nutritious and versatile addition to any recipe. Store pumpkin, sunflower, and hemp seeds in the refrigerator.

Sesame seeds: Black and white sesame seeds are high in an abundance of minerals, and make dishes—both savory and sweet—pop with their undersized-almond appearance and contrasting hue. Due to sesame seeds' high oil content, they have a tendency to turn rancid quickly, making refrigeration necessary.

Tahini: A seed butter made from ground sesame seeds, you may recognize tahini

from its starring role in hummus. Look for a traditional Lebanese variety—its silkiness and earthy flavor are unmatched. After stirring vigorously, store in the refrigerator.

Walnuts: Walnuts can be used on top of oatmeal, toasted and tossed in a salad, chopped and added to pasta for crunch, or eaten out of hand as a snack. Store walnuts in the refrigerator or freezer.

SWEETENERS

Agave nectar: Made from the juice of the same succulent plant that tequila is derived from. Agave nectar has a smooth, clean taste, and works wonderfully as a multi-purpose, natural sweetener. I choose this when I don't want the flavor of the sweetener to overpower the recipe.

Birch syrup : Made from the sap tapped from birch trees, birch syrup is produced in a similar fashion to maple syrup. However, the taste is rich and molasses-like, not having the same super-sweet undertones as maple syrup. Perfect in savory or sweet dishes, such as salad dressings, glazes for tofu, or as a topper for thick, plain yogurt. As it's more expensive and assertive in flavor, I use birch syrup sparingly. Store birch syrup in the refrigerator.

Coconut sugar (granulated): Derived from the sap of the coconut tree, coconut sugar is most similar in taste to brown sugar with caramel undertones. Coconut sugar can be used cup-for-cup in place of any other granulated sugar.

Evaporated cane sugar (granulated): The closest in taste and texture you'll come to white sugar without the refining. Cane sugar juice is evaporated, causing it to crystallize. The environmental impact is smaller compared to that of white sugar, which is reason enough to give it a try.

Honey: Lush and floral, honey can be used in any recipe calling for a liquid sweetener. Play around with different honey varieties, as each region will produce a unique flavor depending on the blossoming flowers in that location.

Maple syrup: I prefer grade-B maple syrup as it has a more complex, bold flavor, but grade-A maple syrup will work equally well in any recipe. The grades are simply an indicator of the time of year they were produced—it has nothing to do with quality. Grade-A maple syrup (light, mild taste) is generally harvested earlier in the season, while grade-B (dark, rich taste) is harvested later in the season. Store maple syrup in the refrigerator.

Medjool dates: These juicy, candy-like dried fruits are multitalented gems in the kitchen. Ideal for "raw" desserts, sweetening smoothies, and can even be chopped up and added to savory grain salads as a sweet foil. I choose dates with the pit intact. If you have celiac disease, make sure the dates aren't coated in flour or cornstarch, which is often contaminated with wheat.

How to Cook from this Book

Along with **The Whole Bowls Formula**, I have a few tips that can help you flawlessly execute your bowls.

PREPARATION TIPS

Weekly greens prep: Greens are some of the most-used ingredients in this book, making prewashing a helpful exercise for quicker-to-the-table meals. I wash kale, herbs, Swiss chard, and other dark leafy or salad greens in water, then dry them in a salad spinner. After drying, I roll the greens up in a paper towel to absorb excess water, preventing mushiness, for storage in a zip-top bag. Not only are the greens ready to use when you need them, this technique also keeps the greens fresher, longer (up to 2 weeks).

Wash before use: With the exception of the greens (mentioned above), most vegetables and fruits should be washed immediately before use (especially berries or they'll turn to mush in your refrigerator). The only produce I don't wash (ever) are mushrooms; instead, I use a paper towel to brush off any dirt.

Storage: While most vegetables and fruits require refrigeration, there are exceptions: winter squashes, potatoes, sweet potatoes, onions, garlic, tomatoes, stone fruits, and bananas should all be kept at room temperature. Avocados and stone fruits can be left at room temperature until perfectly ripe before refrigerating for up to 1 week.

Bringing limp produce back to life: Whether you've left it too long in the refrigerator or it got old faster than you anticipated, you can generally save your less-than-perfect produce with a quick shock in ice water. Carrots, radishes, greens, cucumbers, and more—I've saved a lot of past-prime produce this way.

COOKING TIPS

Read through the entire recipe before beginning: Most recipes in this book have multiple steps, so reading through the recipe in its entirety before cooking is a good idea.

While one component is cooking, get working on another: For instance, if you're cooking a grain for 45 minutes, use that time to cook the vegetables and/or prepare the sauce or dressing for the rest of the bowl.

Read the Make Ahead tips: Employ the *Make Ahead* components of the dish as often as possible so the meals can be assembled when you're in a hurry. Many of the components can be made a few days ahead and some can even be frozen.

Read the Notes: This is where you'll find switch-up and mix-and-match suggestions.

Warm the bowl: A restaurant trick I use every day. If the dish is to be served hot, make sure to warm the bowl to take the chill off. I'm pretty adamant about this in my kitchen, especially for pasta. To warm, use a warming drawer (in some ovens), a low oven (for just a minute), run hot tap water over the dish (dry before use), or fill with a bit of water and heat in the microwave for 15 to 20 seconds (drain water and dry before use).

Use The Whole Bowls Formula to create your own meal: If you don't like a component I've used or simply don't have it handy, don't go running off to the store—you can replace the component with something that better suits your taste and mood.

The Whole Bowls Formula

Something I felt very strongly about while writing this cookbook was giving you, the reader and cook, an opportunity to create your own **Whole Bowl** using the variety of mini recipes found throughout these pages.

If a bowl I've devised doesn't quite ignite an immediacy to make it right this second (which is what I'm aiming for), you can absolutely manipulate and play with the flavors, textures, components, and best of all, seasonality of the bowls to better suit you, as well as your diners.

This formula is a lifesaver when it comes to unexpected guests, many of whom will undoubtedly have different palates and dietary preferences. Assembling a few of the quick-cooking vegetables on the spot, keeping a dressing or sauce at the ready for the week (many freeze beautifully, too), a quick vegetarian protein (canned and dry chickpeas last a lifetime in the pantry), some fresh greens (there are few things faster than a clamshell pack of spinach), a grain (brown rice can be frozen), and perhaps some seeds for a little crunch, and you've got a **Whole Bowl** that will please any diner. No swinging from chandeliers is required for making one up—if it tastes good to you, it's worth eating.

Also, with the dozens of mini recipes found within the recipes themselves (for sauces, grains, proteins, and more), it's really very hard to grow tired of your lunches. Most of the dishes and components are packable, so don't be shy about building a "bowl" in a container to take with you to work, school, or day tripping.

The Whole Bowls Formula is ideal for children and teens, too. If they're too young to be near the heat of the stove or sharp knives, they can assemble their own bowls at the counter or on the table; just lay out the components and they can mix and match. Also, the cooked and cooled vegetable components make excellent finger food for little ones. Prepared grains, beans, condiments, and vegetables stored in clear containers in the refrigerator are perfect for tweens and teens after school; or get them to assemble it for a packable school lunch in lieu of cafeteria food.

Not that you need me to tell you how to build a bowl—this chapter is all about creativity, after all—but I've devised a formula with proportions if you need a helping hand to get started.

GREAT BOWLS START HERE: IT'S ALL IN THE DETAILS

Cooking: Vegetables, grains, and plant-based proteins can turn people off if not cooked correctly. The more you work with them, the more your healthy cooking intuition will develop. It's surprising how different an overcooked piece of broccoli can taste in comparison to a tender-crisp piece of the same plant.

Seasoning: I will be the first to admit that many vegetables, fruits, grains, and plant-based proteins need a little help in the seasoning department. Don't be afraid to season to taste. Because you're working with whole foods, you're in complete control of the salt and sugar—one of the many benefits of cooking with unprocessed food. You don't always have to stick to plain salt, as there are various alternatives you can use to boost the briny brightness it delivers with an added layer of flavor, like olives, cheeses, tamari, miso, pickles, and capers.

Along with salt, a bit of sugar can turn a dish from flat to extraordinary. To build in flavor, try sweeteners such as maple syrup, honey, and dried fruit. A touch of sugar goes a long way, elevating a dish to restaurant-quality cuisine.

And, allow me to introduce you to your new best friend for flavorful bowls: the spice cupboard. I stock up on a variety of dried herbs and spices at my local bulk food store, along with the bulk section of the supermarket. As well as being the most economical purchasing method, it's a way to try small quantities of new tastes you may have previously shied away from. Dried herbs and spices are a quick way to change the theme of a bowl, too. Dried dill can be a nod to Greek cuisine, cumin to Mexican, and cardamom to Scandinavian, to name just a few. Planning meals and dinner parties around a country's flavor profile using just one or two dried herbs or spices is an easy way to take your bowls to the next level (with no extra work).

Texture: If you do go free-range and whip up your own bowl (which I completely encourage), keep texture in mind. A great meal has contrasting textures—snappy, crisp, soft, silken, tender, and crunchy. This makes for the most satisfying, visually appealing, and tasty creations.

Color: A big bowl of beige is not appetizing, full stop. Eating is a multi-sensory experience. How a dish looks to the eyes is just as, or nearly as, important to the taste. Try to stick with two to four different colors or you may end up with something equally as unappetizing as a plain beige dish. If your meal is looking a touch anemic, edible garnishes, such as a scattering of fresh herbs, sprinkle of pumpkin seeds, peppering of pomegranate arils, thread of olive oil, tumble of berries, or twist of lemon zest are all brilliant quick fixes, some doubling as texture boosters to boot.

Condiments
2 tbsp–¼ cup

Crunch or
Garnish
1–2 tbsp

Protein
½ cup
3–4 ounces

Cheese optional
1–2 tbsp
1 ounce

Starchy Vegetables or
Fruit
½ cup–1 cup

Grains
½ cup

Non-Starchy
Vegetables
1–2 cups

The Whole Bowls Formula

THE WHOLE BOWLS FORMULA

Construct a meal that tastes great to you, or construct a meal to use up leftover components you have kicking around. Not every part is mandatory; however, if you feel like going fully loaded, I wholeheartedly support that. If you want to pick a cuisine to theme your bowl around, such as Greek, Italian, Moroccan, or Japanese, that's a great start. Or, if you just want to go rogue and create a never-before-seen proprietary cuisine, that works as well.

Grains: *½ cup*
Keep it simple using plain brown rice or quinoa, or try any number of the more complex (but still very easy) grain-based recipes found in these pages.

Protein: *½ cup or 3–4 ounces*
I recommend chickpeas, hummus, or black beans if you're in a hurry (or even if you're not), but a poached egg, marinated or plain tofu, or tempeh are equally nice to give your bowl some staying power.

Non-Starchy Vegetables: *1–2 cups*
Kale, spinach, radicchio, arugula, bok choy, and more, non-starchy vegetables add color, great taste, and wholesomeness to a bowl. Leftover non-starchy grilled vegetables, like peppers, zucchini, and onions, add a lot of flavor, too.

Starchy Vegetables and/or Fruit: *½ cup– 1 cup*
Roasted sweet potatoes or beets, grated carrots, or tender cubes of butternut squash are a few of my favorites. You'll find many simple recipes for these vegetables in the following pages. Or, if it's fruit season, a tumble of blueberries finds itself quite at home on top of cooked quinoa with diced cucumber and feta.

Condiments: *2 tablespoons–¼ cup*
Condiments perk up every other component, seasoning and enriching a bowl to bring it to life. When combined, balsamic, tamari, and olive oil make a brilliant, quick vinaigrette, but of course, this book is chock-full of more elaborate suggestions—there are dozens upon dozens in the pages ahead. Choose the condiment's consistency in accordance with the other components. For instance, delicate vegetables and lettuces go with lighter oil and vinegar-based dressings, while sturdier, grain-based dishes and starchy vegetables can stand up to a gravy, rich sauce, or creamy dressing.

Crunch and/or Garnish: *1–2 tablespoons*
A touch of crunch adds character to each bite. Try roasted hazelnuts, pumpkin seeds, pomegranate arils, or croutons. I'm especially fond of chopped walnuts in pasta dishes. Crunch can also double as garnish; try chopped fresh herbs, a whisper of a vibrantly hued spice, or a fan of fresh fruit. I prefer to keep my garnishes edible and encourage you to do the same.

Cheese (optional): *1–2 tablespoons or 1 ounce*
Cheese can act as a protein component, seasoning, subtle accent, or all of the above, depending on the dish and amount used. By adding fresh goat cheese, feta, parmesan, and more—if you include cheese in your diet—I think you'll find a quite delightful bowl. As cheese is quite strong, keep it on the lighter side as to not overpower the other components.

Chapter 1: Breakfast Whole Bowls

Eating breakfast out of a bowl is a globally shared experience. North Americans and cold cereal (or smoothie bowls), Irish and steel-cut oats, Japanese and savory rice bowls, Danish and grød—I could go on for nearly the length of this book! We humans are a delicate bunch in the morning, no matter what side of the world we wake up on. We don't want to stray too far from the familiar, yet crave a change in our dining rotation when our unvaried breakfast routine becomes predictable and monotonous.

Breakfast is the only meal I can think of where the images of what it should and could be are so completely dissimilar depending on whom you ask. So, I've constructed the bowls in this chapter for this exact anomaly. There's something in here for the hot grain breakfasters, the savory egg-based breakfast club (and the savory non-egg-based breakfast club), the granola and yogurt devotees, the hurried muesli crowd (wake up, eat a fully prepared morning meal, dash to work), the vegetables in the morning variety, and the brunch-goers.

Because mornings can be frenzied, many of the recipes can be made ahead. You can even entertain with breakfast. Short of growing and milling grains for oatmeal yourself, the following breakfast recipes will impress anyone lucky enough to taste your fine cooking. And, you can cook with the seasons or choose what you're craving now, as I find much of the produce used in this chapter is perpetually at hand these days.

Breakfast bowls are your breezy morning taste bud calisthenics, free of the drama that lunches, dinners, and desserts can bring. Nevertheless, breakfast is still very worthy of a little glitz, flourish, and precision when the time feels right to do so—after all, who says you can't eat your oatmeal out of a fine china bowl? Breakfast sets the tone for the entire day, which is why I encourage you to eat it, but there's absolutely no edict about where it should be eaten, or when (breakfast for dinner, anyone?). Packing breakfast to eat at work is equally appropriate to eating breakfast and leisurely flipping through the news at the table, or standing at the counter chewing and checking your email.

Whatever your morning ritual includes, however groggy-headed you may be, if you're a coffee drinker or tea drinker, a night owl or early bird, one of these breakfast bowls will be well worth planting your feet on the ground for another day. If you choose the nursery coziness of warm grains, satisfy your inner epicurean with a cherry hazelnut pesto swirled into a snow bank of yogurt, or get your taste buds to stand to attention with a heady, crimson shakshuka, I do hope you'll find they're worthy of at least one meal of your day, be that at sunrise or sunset. Eating for pleasure is a key principle of *Whole Bowls*, and the thought of waking up to a hearty bowl of breakfast is very pleasing to me indeed.

BREAKFAST WHOLE BOWLS

PEAR MUESLI WITH FIGS

37

OAT RISOTTO WITH SOFT-BOILED EGGS, AVOCADO,
AND HAZELNUT DUKKAH

39

YOGURT BOWLS WITH CHERRY PESTO
AND HAZELNUT OIL-TOASTED OATS

40

BLACK RICE COCONUT PORRIDGE WITH TOASTED
COCONUT AND PINEAPPLE

42

SHAKSHUKA BREAKFAST BOWLS WITH SOCCA

44

BRUNCH BOWLS WITH CHICKPEA TURNIP HASH, ASPARAGUS,
EGGS, AND HOMEMADE KETCHUP

45

DANISH GRØD WITH CARDAMOM BERRIES

47

BREAKFAST WALDORF WITH MILLET PORRIDGE

49

SWEET POTATO BREAKFAST WITH GINGERBREAD PECAN CRISP

51

TOASTED COCONUT CHIA PUDDING

53

MAPLE ALMOND GRANOLA WITH YOGURT

55

SOUTHERN CHEDDAR GRITS WITH TOMATOES,
KALE, AND BLACK BEANS

57

PEAR MUESLI WITH FIGS

I developed this recipe as a personal challenge. After having the best muesli in the world (well, in my opinion) several years ago at a hotel on the West Coast, I've been trying to figure out the recipe in my own kitchen. It's taken me many years and countless batches of inedible muesli, but I think I've finally done it. Make it the night before and enjoy it for nearly a work-week's worth of no-fuss breakfasts at home, or pack it up to eat at your desk.

As voluptuous, velvet-coated fresh figs seem to be one of the last fruits to still have a noticeable season at stores and markets, replace them when unavailable with any soft-fleshed fruit that appeals to you. I recommend something with an acidic edge; berries, peaches, and plums are ideal substitutions.

Serves 4

For the Pear Muesli

1 cup whole milk plain yogurt (not Greek)

1 cup water

2 tablespoons lemon juice

2 tablespoons maple syrup

½ teaspoon vanilla extract

1 ripe pear, grated

2 cups large flake rolled oats (not instant)

1 cup walnut halves, chopped

¼ cup raisins or dried cranberries (optional)

½ teaspoon sea salt

For Serving

8 fresh figs, halved

MAKE AHEAD

Pear Muesli: 1 week.

Make the Pear Muesli: In a large bowl, combine yogurt, water, lemon juice, maple syrup, and vanilla. Stir in remaining muesli ingredients, mixing well to combine. Cover and refrigerate overnight.

To Serve: To bowls, add muesli; top with figs. Serve.

OAT RISOTTO WITH SOFT-BOILED EGGS, AVOCADO, AND HAZELNUT DUKKAH

It can be a bit of a mental hurdle to think of oats as a tarpaulin for savory flavors; however, their subtle, natural sweetness and mildness can take a heavy-handed application of what are traditionally thought of as "dinner spices." I've paired the classic risotto grain, arborio, with tawny steel-cut oats as this bowl's base. Dukkah, an Egyptian dried condiment made of nuts and spices, along with buttery, chartreuse avocado, and a golden-cored soft-boiled egg all land gleefully on top of this pillowy cloud of grains.

Serves 4, with extra Hazelnut Dukkah

For the Oat Risotto

1 tablespoon unsalted butter

1 cup steel-cut oats

½ cup white arborio rice

1 teaspoon sea salt

3 cups unsweetened plain almond milk

2 cups water

For the Hazlenut Dukkah

¼ cup sesame seeds

½ cup roasted hazelnuts (see page **206**)

2 teaspoons coriander seeds

¼ teaspoon sea salt

For Serving

4 large eggs

2 avocados, halved, pitted, and sliced into thin pieces

extra-virgin olive oil

pea sprouts or sunflower sprouts (optional)

lemon wedges

MAKE AHEAD

Oat Risotto: 1 week. Reheat with additional almond milk to return it to its creamy consistency.

Hazelnut Dukkah: 2 months.

NOTES

Use leftover Hazelnut Dukkah on avocado toast, warm grains, tofu, beans, yogurt, or to garnish hummus.

Make the Oat Risotto: In a large pot or high-sided skillet, warm butter over medium heat until foamy. Add oats, rice, and salt; toast, stirring constantly, for 1–2 minutes. Stir in almond milk and water. Bring to a boil, reduce to medium, and cook, uncovered, stirring every few minutes or so, for 22–25 minutes. (Lower heat in last 10 minutes of cooking time to avoid scorching or splatters if necessary.)

Make the Hazelnut Dukkah: In a skillet, toast sesame seeds over medium heat until tanned (30 seconds–1 minute); add to a food processor with remaining dukkah ingredients, and pulse until finely chopped. Transfer to a glass jar or airtight container for storing in refrigerator.

Make the soft-boiled eggs: Fill a medium saucepan halfway with water; bring to a boil, reduce heat to a rapid simmer, and gently add eggs. Cook for 5–6 minutes, drain immediately, and run cold tap water over shells. Cool for 1 minute. Carefully remove shell.

To Serve: To bowls, add a bed of risotto; top with avocado, egg (halved), and dukkah. Drizzle with oil and garnish with sprouts (if using). Serve with lemon wedges for seasoning.

YOGURT BOWLS WITH CHERRY PESTO AND HAZELNUT OIL-TOASTED OATS

There's really nothing quite as satisfying as embracing your inner flower child and serving yourself a snowy mountain of yogurt for breakfast. Because I couldn't just have a recipe for a plain bowl of yogurt, I give you: fruit pesto. While delightful on its own, it does need something creamy as an anchor, which is where that tangy yogurt comes in. For the final flourish, hazelnut oil is used to toast oats, adding another nutty layer to this celebratory bowl of goodies.

Serves 2–4

For the Hazelnut Oil-Toasted Oats

1 tablespoon roasted hazelnut oil or extra-virgin olive oil

½ cup large flake rolled oats (not instant)

½ teaspoon ground cinnamon

¼ teaspoon sea salt

For the Cherry Pesto

½ cup roasted hazelnuts (see page **206**)

1 tablespoon coconut sugar or evaporated cane sugar

½ teaspoon cinnamon

2 cups frozen, defrosted, unsweetened, dark pitted cherries or fresh cherries, pitted

2 teaspoons lemon juice or balsamic vinegar

For the Yogurt

2 cups plain Greek yogurt

1 tablespoon maple syrup

1 teaspoon vanilla extract or vanilla bean paste

Make the Hazelnut Oil-Toasted Oats: In a large skillet, warm oil over medium heat. Add oats, cinnamon, and salt. Toast, stirring often for 3–5 minutes, until fragrant. Transfer to a small bowl.

Make the Cherry Pesto: In a food processor, pulse hazelnuts, sugar, and cinnamon until finely chopped. Add cherries and lemon juice, briefly blending until mostly smooth, leaving a little texture.

Make the Yogurt: In a medium bowl, mix all yogurt ingredients. Cover and refrigerate until ready to serve.

To Serve: To bowls, add yogurt; swirl in pesto and sprinkle generously with oats. Serve.

MAKE AHEAD

Cherry Pesto: 1 week.

Yogurt: 1 week.

Hazelnut Oil-Toasted Oats: 1 month.

BLACK RICE COCONUT PORRIDGE WITH TOASTED COCONUT AND PINEAPPLE

Also known as forbidden rice, this black-tie grain stays gorgeously glossy and raven, even when diluted with antithetically colored coconut milk. Cooked much like rice pudding, it looks very special occasion, yet couldn't be easier. Hit with a few complimentary tastes of the tropics, this bowl is as pleasing to the eye as it is to the palate. Replace pineapple with mango for a similar bumblebee color scheme, or try kiwi (which may look a bit Halloweeny, but still very tasty), papaya, or good ol' bananas.

.... *Serves 4* ....

For the Black Rice Coconut Porridge

1 cup black rice

3 cups water

1 (14-ounce) can full-fat coconut milk

3 tablespoons coconut sugar

1 teaspoon vanilla extract

½ teaspoon ground dried ginger

½ teaspoon sea salt

For the Toasted Coconut

½ cup unsweetened coconut flakes or unsweetened shredded coconut

For Serving

pineapple, cored and cut into ½-inch pieces

ground nutmeg

1 lime, quartered

Make the Black Rice Coconut Porridge: In a large pot, combine all porridge ingredients. Bring to a boil, reduce to medium, and cook, uncovered, for 40–50 minutes, stirring often.

Make the Toasted Coconut: To a large nonstick skillet, add coconut, toasting over medium heat for 1–2 minutes until light brown; immediately transfer to a plate.

To Serve: To bowls, add porridge; top with pineapple, toasted coconut, and nutmeg. Serve with lime for seasoning.

> **MAKE AHEAD**
>
> *Black Rice Coconut Porridge:* 2 days. Reheat with additional milk or water to return it to its creamy consistency.
>
> *Toasted Coconut:* 6 months.

SHAKSHUKA BREAKFAST BOWLS WITH SOCCA

Shakshuka—a heady, spiced tomato sauce canvas that burbles away while slowly poaching eggs—is as delicious as it is delightful to say. Here, I've accompanied the pepper-spiked gravy with socca, a savory chickpea flour skillet pancake, helping to sop up some of that vibrant sauce. It's an extravagant meal that works well as a leisurely weekend breakfast or weeknight dinner.

Serves 4

For the Socca (chickpea pancake)

2 cups chickpea (garbanzo) flour

1 teaspoon sea salt

2 cups water

1 tablespoon extra-virgin olive oil

1 tablespoon coconut oil or refined avocado oil

For the Shakshuka

3 tablespoons extra-virgin olive oil

1 onion, thinly sliced into half-moons

1 red bell pepper, cored and thinly sliced into strips

2 cloves garlic, minced

1½ teaspoons ground cumin

1 teaspoon sea salt

½ teaspoon mild smoked or sweet paprika

½ teaspoon whole caraway seeds

⅛ teaspoon cayenne

1 (28-ounce) can whole tomatoes

4 large eggs

Make the Socca: Leave oven rack in middle (normal) position. Heat broiler to 400°F (usually its lowest setting). In a large bowl, combine flour and salt; whisk in water and olive oil until smooth. Allow to sit at room temperature for a few minutes. Heat a 9-inch cast-iron or ovenproof nonstick skillet over medium; add coconut oil, swirling to coat bottom, and pour in batter. Broil for 5 minutes, turn off broiler; leave in oven for 5 minutes longer until browned and completely set. Carefully remove from oven (handle is very hot!). Slice into wedges directly in pan or slide onto cutting board to slice.

Make the Shakshuka: Preheat oven to 375°F. In a large, ovenproof, high-sided skillet, warm oil over medium-low heat. Add onion and bell pepper; cook slowly for 20 minutes. Add garlic, cumin, salt, paprika, caraway, and cayenne; cook for 2 minutes longer. Add tomatoes, breaking up large pieces with spoon. Bring to a boil, reduce to a simmer, cover, and cook for 10 minutes. Remove from heat and carefully crack eggs directly into sauce. Bake for 10–15 minutes, until whites are set and yolks still have some jiggle.

To Serve: To bowls, add shakshuka and eggs; nestle in a wedge of socca or serve on the side. Serve.

> **MAKE AHEAD**
>
> *Socca:* 3 days.
>
> *Shakshuka (sauce only, without eggs):* 1 week; 2 months, frozen.

BRUNCH BOWLS WITH CHICKPEA TURNIP HASH, ASPARAGUS, EGGS, AND HOMEMADE KETCHUP

Dilled, peppery turnips and chickpea marbles replace the common potato, acting as groundwork for this midmorning repast. Asparagus is the greenery, and eggs bring their emblematic, canary-colored clout. The ketchup recipe makes a lot, but can be stored in jars and frozen, employed anywhere you'd normally add it beyond this bowl (veggie burgers, macaroni and cheese, etc.).

Serves 4–5, with plenty of leftover Homemade Ketchup

For the Homemade Ketchup

1 (28-ounce) can whole tomatoes

1 (5.5-ounce) can tomato paste

1 onion, diced

¼ cup distilled white vinegar

1 tablespoon honey

2 teaspoons sea salt

¼ teaspoon ground cloves (do not skip this—it's the "secret ingredient" in commercial ketchup)

ground black pepper, to taste

For the Bowls

2 tablespoons extra-virgin olive oil

2 turnips, peeled and diced into small cubes (same size as chickpeas)

1 onion, chopped

2 teaspoons dried dill

1 teaspoon sea salt

ground black pepper, to taste

⅛ teaspoon cayenne pepper

2 cups cooked chickpeas

1 tablespoon lemon juice

1 pound asparagus, tough ends trimmed, cut into 1-inch pieces (leave some water clinging)

For Serving

4–8 eggs (depending on hunger level/number of diners), cooked any way you like (fried, scrambled, etc.)

MAKE AHEAD

Chickpea Turnip Hash: 3 days.

Homemade Ketchup: 1 month; 2 months, frozen (freezing in 1-cup portions is recommended).

Make the Homemade Ketchup: In a large pot, combine all ketchup ingredients. Bring to a boil, reduce to a simmer, cover, and cook for 20 minutes, until onions are tender. Add to a blender or food processor (or use an immersion blender off the heat) and purée until smooth.

Make the Bowls: Preheat oven to 400°F.

For the hash, in a large high-sided skillet, warm oil over medium heat. Add turnips, onion, dill, salt, pepper, and cayenne; sauté for 12–15 minutes, until turnips and onions begin to brown. Add chickpeas and lemon juice; sauté for 5 minutes longer.

For the asparagus, add to a large-rimmed baking sheet. Roast in preheated oven for 10 minutes. Alternatively, steam asparagus for 3–5 minutes.

To Serve: Cook eggs immediately before serving. To bowls, add hash, asparagus, and eggs; top with ketchup or serve on the side. Serve.

DANISH GRØD WITH CARDAMOM BERRIES

Grød is Denmark's interpretation of porridge. Rolled oats and chia seeds are gently cooked in almond milk, doing double duty as nursery-soothing aromatherapy. (And yes, I've spiked the oats with kelp power, but it's completely optional—I'm just a big fan of the nutritional prowess of sea vegetables.) To perfume the berries sitting happily on top of the oats, I've used the classic Scandinavian spice, cardamom, giving cinnamon the morning off. The berries are sweetened with birch syrup, another Scandinavian ingredient, but feel free to use maple syrup or molasses for the same effect.

Serves 2

For the Grød

2 cups unsweetened plain almond milk

⅔ cup large flake rolled oats (not instant)

¼ teaspoon sea salt

1 tablespoon chia seeds (substituting or omitting is not recommended, as they thicken the porridge)

¼ teaspoon kelp or dulse powder or granules (optional)

For the Cardamom Berries

1 cup mixed berries, fresh or frozen

2 teaspoons birch syrup

¼ teaspoon ground cardamom

Topping Suggestions

nuts or seeds of choice

Booster Topping (see page **208**)

1–2 tablespoons nut butter (see page **205**)

banana slices

plain yogurt or buttermilk

> **MAKE AHEAD**
>
> *Cardamom Berries:* 3 days.

Make the Grød: In a medium saucepan, combine milk, oats, and salt. Bring to a boil, reduce to medium-low, and cook, stirring often for 5 minutes. Stir in chia seeds and kelp or dulse; cook, stirring often for 3–5 minutes longer until porridge has thickened.

Make the Cardamom Berries: In a small saucepan, combine berries, birch syrup, and cardamom, cover, and cook over medium heat, until berries are softened and warm (3–5 minutes).

To Serve: To a bowl, add oats; spoon over berries and any of the suggested toppings. Serve.

BREAKFAST WALDORF WITH MILLET PORRIDGE

Grinding whole millet in a blender creates a type of "cream of millet" hot cereal experience that cooks in mere minutes. The barely tanned bowl of creamed grains, while cozy, needs crunch, brightness, and something juicy. Enter: the breakfast waldorf (stick with me here, there is no mayonnaise in this recipe). Salad doesn't need to be savory to be classified as such, which is why it just feels right on this warm/cold bowl.

Serves 3–4

For the Waldorf

2 heaping cups red or green seedless grapes, halved

1 apple or 1 pear, cored and diced

1 cup walnuts, chopped

2 tablespoons dried currants or raisins

1 cup whole milk plain yogurt

1 tablespoon lemon juice

For the Millet Porridge

1 cup millet

1 tablespoon unsalted butter or coconut oil

3¾ cups water or a combination of water and almond milk

¾ teaspoon sea salt

MAKE AHEAD

Waldorf: 3 days.

Millet Porridge: 1 week. Reheat with a splash of water or almond milk to return it to its creamy consistency.

NOTES

For a single serving: 1 teaspoon butter or coconut oil, ¼ cup ground millet, 1¼ cups water or almond milk, and ¼ teaspoon sea salt; follow same cooking directions as above.

Make the Waldorf: In a large bowl, combine all salad ingredients.

Make the Millet Porridge: In a blender or food processor, blend/pulse millet into a course flour. In a large high-sided skillet or pot, melt butter over medium heat. Add millet and toast for 2 minutes, followed by water and salt. Whisking constantly, bring to a boil, reduce to a simmer, partially cover, and cook, whisking often, for 8–10 minutes.

To Serve: To bowls, add porridge; top with waldorf. Serve.

SWEET POTATO BREAKFAST WITH GINGERBREAD PECAN CRISP

Vegetables gussied up for breakfast. Yes, I went there. If you're curious and/or skeptical of a sweet potato cavorting about in your breakfast bowl, all the more reason to try it, I say.

Serves 4, with extra Gingerbread Pecan Crisp

For the Gingerbread Pecan Crisp

⅓ cup coconut oil, melted

⅓ cup orange juice

2 tablespoons molasses

2 cups large flake rolled oats (not instant)

½ cup pecan halves, roughly chopped

1 tablespoon dark buckwheat flour

2 teaspoons ground dried ginger

1 teaspoon ground cinnamon

½ teaspoon sea salt

For the Bowls

4 small or 2 large sweet potatoes, well-scrubbed

2 teaspoons coconut oil

¼ cup crème fraîche or whole milk plain yogurt

zest of 1 orange

orange wedges

maple syrup or dark brown sugar

MAKE AHEAD

Sweet Potatoes: 4 days.

Gingerbread Pecan Crisp: 1 month.

Make the Gingerbread Pecan Crisp: Preheat oven to 300°F. Line a large-rimmed baking sheet with parchment paper. In a large bowl, combine oil, orange juice, and molasses. Mix in remaining ingredients. Spread evenly onto prepared baking sheet and bake for 40–50 minutes, until uniformly browned. Cool completely on baking sheet before storing in an airtight container or jar in the pantry.

Make the Bowls: Preheat oven to 400°F. Line a baking sheet with parchment paper. Add sweet potatoes and rub skins with oil; prick a few times with a knife. Bake for 45 minutes to 1 hour, or until very tender and beginning to caramelize. Cool for 10 minutes.

To Serve: To bowls, add sweet potatoes, cutting lengthwise down the center, opening to create a "bowl," or use half a large potato. Dollop with crème fraîche or yogurt, and top with crumble and orange zest. Serve with orange wedges and maple syrup or brown sugar.

TOASTED COCONUT CHIA PUDDING

Chia seeds have so much goodness in them (iron, fiber, and protein, to name a few), yet I've been challenged by their texture for years. It was a deeply personal undertaking that I create a chia pudding that I could not only stand, but crave—and I think I've done just that. Helping matters out is coconut, an ingredient that I could quickly turn into a magnum opus thanks to how much and how often I use it in my kitchen, along with a selection of other tropical delights. Nutty, floral, and naturally sweet coconut flakes give textural contrast, while slightly sour, sunshiny tropical fruit act as the garnish.

As the pudding has to chill in the refrigerator to set for a few hours, make this the evening before and wake up to a premade breakfast.

Serves 4

For the Chia Pudding
1 cup unsweetened plain almond milk
1 cup full-fat coconut milk (thick, canned)

2 tablespoons maple syrup
1 teaspoon lime juice
1 teaspoon vanilla extract
pinch, sea salt
⅓ cup chia seeds

For Serving
⅓ cup unsweetened coconut flakes or shredded coconut
2 cups cubed tropical fruit (dragonfruit, mango, pineapple, etc.)

MAKE AHEAD

Chia Pudding:
1 week.

Toasted Coconut:
6 months.

Make the Chia Pudding: In a large bowl, whisk together all pudding ingredients except chia seeds. Whisk in chia seeds; continue to whisk for 1 minute. Rest at room temperature for 20 minutes, whisking every so often. Cover and chill for at least 3 hours (overnight best).

Make the toasted coconut: To a large nonstick skillet, add coconut, toasting over medium for 1–2 minutes until light brown. Immediately transfer to a plate.

To Serve: Stir pudding vigorously. To bowls, add chilled pudding; top with fruit and toasted coconut. Serve.

MAPLE ALMOND GRANOLA WITH YOGURT

There is something so satisfying about granola, fruit, and yogurt. It's one of those meals I could (and often do) eat for any meal or snack of the day. After experimenting with several granola-baking techniques, I've discovered a low and slow bake results in the crispiest, sweetest (non-burnt) granola. It does spend nearly an hour in the oven, but your patience will be rewarded as it makes a large batch to carry you through a week or so of homemade breakfasts.

Makes about 4 cups Maple Almond Granola

For the Maple Almond Granola

⅓ cup coconut oil, melted
⅓ cup maple syrup
2 teaspoons vanilla extract

3 cups large flake rolled oats (not instant)
1 cup raw almonds, roughly chopped
2 teaspoons ground cinnamon
½ teaspoon sea salt

For Serving
plain yogurt
fresh fruit
almond milk

MAKE AHEAD

Maple Almond Granola: 1 month.

NOTES

Replace almonds with walnuts or pecans, or try pumpkin seeds for a nut-free variation.

Make the Maple Almond Granola: Preheat oven to 300°F. Line a large-rimmed baking sheet with parchment paper. In a large bowl, combine coconut oil, maple syrup, and vanilla. Mix in remaining ingredients. Spread evenly onto prepared baking sheet and bake for 55 minutes–1 hour, until uniformly browned. Cool completely on baking sheet before storing in an airtight container or jar in the pantry.

To Serve: To a bowl, add yogurt and granola; top with fruit. Serve with almond milk.

SOUTHERN CHEDDAR GRITS WITH TOMATOES, KALE, AND BLACK BEANS

While spending a food-filled long weekend in New Orleans, Louisiana, I fell in love with creamy, comforting grits. The food culture in Louisiana runs deep. From cab drivers to the friendliest high-end kitchen teams, everyone wanted to chat about food—I was in my element! Taking a page from the chefs and home cooks down South, I've added a sharp cheddar cheese and spiced the beans with a creole blend. Every time I need a taste of the warm and welcoming South (usually in the depths of a Canadian winter), I whip up this savory breakfast bowl.

Serves 1

For the Cheddar Grits

1½ cups water

¼ cup white hominy grits (smooth and creamy old fashioned, not instant)

½ teaspoon sea salt

coarsely ground black pepper, to taste, plus more for serving

1½ ounces (heaping ¼ cup) grated old white cheddar

1 cup de-stemmed, chopped kale

For the Black Beans

½ cup cooked black beans

1 teaspoon apple cider vinegar

¼ teaspoon creole seasoning

sea salt, to taste

For Serving

½ cup–1 cup cocktail or cherry tomatoes, halved

extra-virgin olive oil or butter

MAKE AHEAD

Black Beans: 2 days.

NOTES

If you can't find grits in store, they're widely available online. Or use coarse polenta in its place.

I always add hot sauce to this bowl. It just feels right.

Make the Cheddar Grits: In a medium saucepan, whisking constantly, bring water, grits, salt, and pepper to a boil, reduce to low, cover, and cook for 15 minutes, whisking often. Whisk in cheddar until melted. Stir in kale, cover, and cook until kale is wilted (1–2 minutes).

Make the Black Beans: In a small bowl, combine all bean ingredients.

To Serve: To a bowl, add grits; top with beans, tomatoes, a thread of olive oil or pat of butter, and sprinkle of pepper. Serve.

Chapter 2: Salad Whole Bowls

Depending on one's definition of the dish, salads can conjure up a multitude of noticeably dissimilar images. The salads appearing in this chapter are meal-sized, stick-to-your-ribs delights, celebrating the symphony of texture, flavors, temperatures, and colors that are my requisite features for a great bowl. While some recipes do have a more traditional base of peppery lettuces, crisp greens that burst with water at first bite, and loud, bitter leaves, others skip the lettuce altogether, replacing these routine bases with delicate grains, slurpable pastas, and creamy beans.

A *Whole Bowls* salad can be based upon seasonal and local ingredients, even in the depths of winter with meltingly tender squashes and root vegetables, now in their prime. Or, if you're a gardener, a salad can be built from the goodies in your own backyard in the muggy heat of summer. And, if you're craving a punchier, international flavor profile, salads can be assembled from pantry saviors, like peanut butter, tamari, and sesame oil, simply accented with crisp, good-year-round produce—with nary a leafy green in sight.

In this chapter, I'm aiming to transform the standard definition of salad, removing the iceberg (although, it has a place in that retro-fabulous blue cheesy wedge) and bottled dressing, to a completely gratifying meal to sit down to solo or with family and friends. The oodles of mini recipes—from dressings to croutons, roasted vegetables to marinated beans— found within the next several pages, can all be employed for use with **The Whole Bowls Formula**. Having a few components prepared throughout the week allows you to have a mini salad bar in your very own kitchen.

The following recipes are what salad ought to be in my mind: a celebration of plants—one that doesn't leave you hungry an hour after eating. For the culinary traditionalists, there are classic salad combinations—with a few twists, of course—to satisfy your craving for the familiar; and, for the food adventurers, a plentitude of international inspiration to pique your appetite. (I fall into both camps, depending on my mood.)

No need to polish the tines of your fork, just dive in heartily, happily, and with a new idea of what salad can be.

SALAD WHOLE BOWLS

BUTTER LETTUCE WITH LEMONY CHICKPEA, RAISIN, QUINOA, AND
SUNFLOWER SEED SALAD
63

WINE COUNTRY SALAD WITH WILD RICE GRAPE PILAF AND HALLOUMI
65

EAT YOUR GREENS SALAD WITH CHICKPEA CROUTONS AND
GREEN GODDESS DRESSING
67

CURRIED FALAFEL WITH KALE SALAD
69

FORBIDDEN RICE SALAD WITH BLACK BEANS,
STICKY SQUASH, AND ARUGULA
70

GADO GADO WITH PLUMS AND PEANUT DRESSING
71

RADICCHIO WITH BEETS, SWEETS, AND CLASSIC
BALSAMIC DRESSING
73

WARM LENTIL SALAD WITH ROASTED PEPPERS
75

PATIO BOWLS WITH SWEET POTATO WEDGES, GRILLED LETTUCE,
AND STICKY BBQ TEMPEH
77

SOUTH OF THE BORDER BOWLS WITH WALNUT MEAT
AND GRILLED AVOCADO
79

YOGURT PASTA SALAD WITH SUNBLUSH TOMATOES AND ZA'ATAR-
MARINATED BUTTER BEANS
81

BUTTER LETTUCE WITH LEMONY CHICKPEA, RAISIN, QUINOA, AND SUNFLOWER SEED SALAD

Delicate butter lettuce mothers a refreshingly light and zingy salad of quinoa, chickpeas, whole lemons, plump raisins, and crispy sunflower seeds. It's all topped with a rather addictive tahini dressing that's been sharpened with a hit of garlic. In lieu of lining your salad bowls with lettuce, the leaves can be employed as a bowl themselves (which means one fewer dish to clean to boot).

Serves 4

For the Salad
¾ cup water
½ cup uncooked quinoa
2 cups cooked chickpeas
¼ cup raisins
¼ cup raw hulled sunflower seeds
zest of 1 lemon

1 whole lemon or 2 meyer lemons, peeled, seeded, and flesh cut into small pieces
1 tablespoon extra-virgin olive oil
½ teaspoon sea salt
ground black pepper, to taste
2 heads butter (Boston, bibb) lettuce, leaves kept whole and separated

Yogurt Tahini Dressing
⅓ cup whole milk plain yogurt
¼ cup tahini
2 tablespoons lemon juice
1 tablespoon water
1 clove garlic, minced
¼ teaspoon sea salt

MAKE AHEAD

Salad: 4 days (without lettuce; add to lettuce-lined bowls and drizzle with dressing immediately before serving).

Yogurt Tahini Dressing: 1 week.

Make the Salad: In a medium saucepan, bring water and quinoa to a boil, reduce to a simmer, cover, and cook for 15 minutes; remove from heat and steam, covered, for 5 minutes. Add cooked quinoa to a large salad bowl along with chickpeas, raisins, sunflower seeds, lemon zest and pieces, oil, salt, and pepper; mix well to combine. Chill for 1 hour, or set aside if serving immediately at room temperature.

Make the Yogurt Tahini Dressing: In a small bowl, whisk all dressing ingredients.

To Serve: Line bowls with butter lettuce leaves; fill center with salad mixture and drizzle with dressing. Serve.

WINE COUNTRY SALAD WITH WILD RICE GRAPE PILAF AND HALLOUMI

This bowl travels well, allowing you to pack up a picnic and head to your local wine country for a bit of al fresco taste of tourism. And, what goes better with wine than cheese? Halloumi, a firm cheese that can be panfried without melting (it's infallible), adorns a salad of bristly stakes of wild rice, sweet grapes, and tender greens. Once the rice is cooked, there's little magicking to be done, so you have ample time to luxuriate in its simple sophistication (and perhaps a glass of wine at lunch).

Serves 4

For the Wild Rice Grape Pilaf

3 cups water

1 cup uncooked wild rice

3 cups red or green seedless grapes, halved

2 cups packed baby spinach

1 cup packed, roughly chopped parsley

4 scallions, minced

2 tablespoons extra-virgin olive oil

2 tablespoons lemon juice

1 tablespoon Dijon mustard

¾ teaspoon sea salt

ground black pepper, to taste

For Serving

1 (8-ounce) package halloumi, cut crosswise into ½-inch slices

MAKE AHEAD

Wild Rice Grape Pilaf: 2 days.

Halloumi: 2 days.

Make the Wild Rice Grape Pilaf: In a medium saucepan, bring water and rice to a boil, reduce to a simmer, cover, and cook for 40–50 minutes, until grains burst; drain. In a large bowl, toss together cooked rice (still warm or chilled, both work), grapes, spinach, parsley, and scallions. In a small bowl, whisk together oil, lemon juice, mustard, salt, and pepper; add to rice mixture, tossing well to combine. Cover and leave at room temperature or refrigerate until ready to serve.

Make the Halloumi: Heat a large nonstick skillet over medium-high. Add halloumi (do not overcrowd pan) and cook 1–2 minutes per side, until golden. Repeat with remaining halloumi, as necessary.

To Serve: To bowls, add a bed of pilaf; top with a few pieces of halloumi. Serve.

EAT YOUR GREENS SALAD WITH CHICKPEA CROUTONS AND GREEN GODDESS DRESSING

Green goddess dressing is a retro recipe straight from the 1920s (nearly one hundred years old now, if you can believe it) first created in San Francisco. While a tad campy and unmodern, it does taste fresh and new with the addition of coconut milk. Crisp chickpea croutons are judiciously doused in smoked paprika, adding dimension and a vibrant color contrast—but making sure not to take away from the verdant extravagance of this bowl's base. The richness of the mayonnaise and coconut milk irons out any wrinkles from the herbs and scallions in terms of sharpness or bitterness.

.... *Serves 4, with leftover Green Goddess Dressing* ....

For the Chickpea Croutons
2 cups cooked chickpeas
1 teaspoon extra-virgin olive oil
1 teaspoon smoked paprika
¼ teaspoon garlic powder
½ teaspoon sea salt
ground black pepper, to taste

For the Green Goddess Dressing (makes 1½ cups)
½ cup mayonnaise (see page **198**)
⅓ cup coconut milk
4 scallions, roughly chopped
½ cup packed fresh parsley
¼ cup packed fresh dill
⅓ cup packed fresh basil

1 tablespoon honey
½ teaspoon sea salt
ground black pepper, to taste

For the Salad
1–2 heads romaine or green leaf lettuce (sizes fluctuate), torn or cut into bite-sized pieces
1 English cucumber, cut into 1-inch cubes

MAKE AHEAD

Green Goddess Dressing: 5 days.

Chickpea Croutons: 1 week.

Briefly reheat in 350°F oven to re-crisp if desired.

Make the Chickpea Croutons: Preheat oven to 400°F. On a large-rimmed baking sheet, mix all crouton ingredients. Bake for 20 minutes.

Make the Green Goddess Dressing: Add all dressing ingredients to a blender or food processor in the order listed. Blend until smooth and uniformly green.

To Serve: In a large salad bowl, toss romaine and cucumber with dressing (use as much as you like). Divide amongst serving bowls; top with chickpea croutons. Serve.

CURRIED FALAFEL WITH KALE SALAD

Falafel are wonderful, deep-fried delights that I could pop like candy. However, I don't own a deep fryer—but I do have an oven! These baked sensations—which acquired the moniker Goldenballs during development—are hit with rich curry, adding spiciness and a faux deep-fried hue. Tahini dressing, a falafel requisite, is imbued with the same sunshiny curry powder, as well as maple syrup, lending a caramel-like sweetness that melds beautifully with a simple salad of kale, carrots, and cucumbers.

.... *Serves 4* ....

For the Curried Falafel

1 tablespoon refined avocado oil or extra-virgin olive oil

1 onion, roughly chopped

2 cloves garlic

2 cups cooked chickpeas

1 tablespoon lemon juice

1 tablespoon curry powder

½ teaspoon sea salt

½ cup chickpea flour

For the Dressing

3 tablespoons tahini

2 tablespoons lemon juice

2 tablespoons water

1 tablespoon maple syrup

1 tablespoon nutritional yeast

2 teaspoons curry powder

½ teaspoon sea salt

ground black pepper, to taste

For the Kale Salad

½ bunch (4–5 cups) kale, destemmed and torn into bite-sized pieces

1 large carrot, julienned or grated

1 regular cucumber, peeled and diced

MAKE AHEAD

Kale Salad (Dressed): 3 days.

Curried Falafel: 4 days; 2 months, frozen.

Dressing: 1 week.

Make the Curried Falafel: Preheat oven to 425°F. Line a large-rimmed baking sheet with parchment paper and grease with oil. In a food processor, pulse onion and garlic until a paste forms. Add chickpeas, lemon juice, curry powder, and salt; pulse until fully combined. Pulse in chickpea flour until fully combined (will look like very thick hummus). Rest for 30–40 minutes at room temperature to allow flour to absorb excess moisture.

Line a large-rimmed baking sheet with parchment paper and grease with oil. Scoop 2–3 tablespoon-sized rounds onto parchment, roll into balls. Bake for 25 minutes.

Make the Dressing: In a small bowl, whisk together all ingredients.

Make the Kale Salad: In a large salad bowl, massage kale until bright green and tender. Add carrots, cucumber, and dressing; toss to combine.

To Serve: To bowls, add a bed of salad; top with a few falafel. Serve.

FORBIDDEN RICE SALAD WITH BLACK BEANS, STICKY SQUASH, AND ARUGULA

While forbidden rice sounds a little bit slinky, it's simply black rice (which appears a few times throughout these pages), now widely available in most major grocery and bulk food stores. Squash adds meatiness and sweetness, while peppery, feathered arugula keeps this out of the overly syrupy category, holding it as lunch appropriate. An ideal fall midday meal.

Serves 4

For the Salad

1 cup water

½ cup black rice

5 ounces (6–8 cups) arugula

2 cups cooked black beans

2 tablespoons flaxseed oil or extra-virgin olive oil

1 tablespoon lemon juice

1 teaspoon ground cumin

1 teaspoon sea salt

ground black pepper, to taste

For the Sticky Squash

1 (2-pound) kabocha or butternut squash, peeled, seeded, and cut into 1-inch cubes

2 tablespoons orange juice

1 tablespoon balsamic vinegar

1 tablespoon extra-virgin olive oil

½ teaspoon sea salt

Make the black rice: In a medium saucepan, bring water and rice to a boil, reduce to a simmer, cover, and cook for 45 minutes. Remove from heat and steam, covered for 5 minutes. Fluff with a fork.

Make the Sticky Squash: Preheat oven to 400°F. Line a large-rimmed baking sheet with parchment paper, add all squash ingredients, toss to combine, and line in a single layer. Bake for 35–40 minutes, until tender.

Make the Salad: In a large salad bowl, toss cooked rice and squash with remaining salad ingredients. Serve.

MAKE AHEAD

Black Rice: 3 days.

Sticky Squash: 3 days.

GADO GADO WITH PLUMS AND PEANUT DRESSING

A traditional Indonesian salad that's perfectly paired with the philosophy of this cookbook, Gado Gado's collection of elements awakens the palate with color, texture, and a range of disparate yet complimentary tastes. While the ingredients can vary, they're typically bound together by sweet-sour-salty-crunchy components and a savory peanut dressing that has just enough saccharinity to make it sing.

Serves 4

For the Gado Gado

4 large eggs

4 cups finely shredded red cabbage

2 cups bean sprouts

1 carrot, shaved with a julienne peeler or grated

1 cucumber, peeled and cubed

1 cup cherry or grape tomatoes, halved

1 cup roughly chopped fresh cilantro

2 black plums, halved, pitted, and sliced

¼ cup roasted peanuts, chopped

For the Peanut Dressing

⅓ cup unsalted natural peanut butter (smooth or crunchy)

1 clove garlic, minced

3 tablespoons water

2 tablespoons lime juice

2 tablespoons tamari

½ teaspoon chili flakes

1 teaspoon coconut sugar or evaporated cane sugar

MAKE AHEAD

Hardboiled Eggs: 1 week.

Peanut Dressing: 2 weeks. Thin with water before serving, as needed (dressing thickens once chilled).

Make the hardboiled eggs: In a medium saucepan, cover eggs with 2 inches of water, bring to a boil, remove from heat, cover, and let sit for 10 minutes; drain, run cold water over eggs, peel, and halve.

Make the Peanut Dressing: In a medium bowl, whisk all dressing ingredients. If you prefer a thinner dressing, add water, 1 tablespoon at a time, until desired consistency.

To Serve: To bowls, add sections of cabbage, sprouts, carrot, cucumber, tomatoes, cilantro, sliced plums, and egg; top with dressing and peanuts. Serve.

RADICCHIO WITH BEETS, SWEETS, AND CLASSIC BALSAMIC DRESSING

Radicchio is bitter, sometimes overwhelmingly so, but I've tamed this dragon with two sweet root vegetables in the form of beets and sweet potatoes. They're starchy and syrupy, almost like candy, playing perfectly off the radicchio's palate-challenging edge. This bowl keeps well for a couple of days, even fully dressed.

························ *Serves 4* ························

For the Salad

1 pound (about 4 small) beets, cut into small cubes

1 pound (about 2 medium) sweet potatoes, cut into small cubes

1 tablespoon extra-virgin olive oil

½ teaspoon sea salt

ground black pepper, to taste

2 heads radicchio, cored and cut lengthwise into wedges

4 ounces feta cheese, sliced crosswise into ½-inch strips (about the size of a domino)

¼ cup chopped pecans

For the Classic Balsamic Dressing

2 tablespoons balsamic vinegar

2 tablespoons roasted hazelnut oil or extra-virgin olive oil

1 clove garlic, minced

1 teaspoon maple syrup

½ teaspoon sea salt

ground black pepper, to taste

MAKE AHEAD

Salad (dressed): 2 days.

Roasted Vegetables: 4 days.

Classic Balsamic Dressing: 1 week.

Make the Salad: Preheat oven to 375°F. On a large-rimmed baking sheet, toss beets and sweet potatoes with oil, salt, and pepper. Roast for 45–55 minutes, until tender.

Make the Classic Balsamic Dressing: In a small bowl (to whisk) or jar (to shake), combine all dressing ingredients.

To Serve: To bowls, add a bed of roasted beets and sweets; top with radicchio, feta, and pecans. Drizzle over dressing. Serve. Or, cut radicchio into bite-sized pieces, add to a large salad bowl along with remaining components and dressing; toss to combine. Serve.

WARM LENTIL SALAD WITH ROASTED PEPPERS

Lentils have an extraordinary earthy taste, satisfying chew, and cook up in less than 30 minutes, but they do need a gentle lift to elevate them. For this, I recommend brightening up most lentil and bean dishes with something acidic—vinegar does the trick here, as do the sweet tangles of roasted peppers. Serve as a main course on a bed of greens or grains, or enjoy as a side salad. Leftovers taste just as nice chilled, too.

Serves 2–4

2 bell peppers, any color, halved, seeded, and sliced into thin strips

2 tablespoons extra-virgin olive oil, divided

1 cup uncooked brown lentils

1 clove garlic, minced

1 tablespoon red wine vinegar

1 teaspoon smoked mild paprika

½ teaspoon sea salt

ground black pepper, to taste

MAKE AHEAD

Warm Lentil Salad with Roasted Peppers: 5 days.

Make the Roasted Peppers: Preheat oven to 400°F. On a large-rimmed baking sheet lined with parchment paper, toss peppers with 1 tablespoon oil. Roast for 40 minutes.

Make the Lentils: In a large pot, add lentils and cover with two inches of water. Bring to a boil, reduce to a simmer, partially cover, and cook for 15–20 minutes, until lentils are tender; drain well.

To Serve: Add lentils back to pot along with roasted peppers, remaining 1 tablespoon oil, garlic, vinegar, paprika, salt, and pepper. Cook, stirring often, over medium heat until heated through and garlic is fragrant. Serve warm or chilled.

PATIO BOWLS WITH SWEET POTATO WEDGES, GRILLED LETTUCE, AND STICKY BBQ TEMPEH

I was betwixt and between about whether this dish should be classified as a salad or entrée. Lettuce screams "salad," so salad it is—but a seasonless one at that. I've even enjoyed this in the winter using an indoor grill pan. Similar to the cataloguing of this recipe, the tempeh here has a bit of an identity crisis; it's coated in a BBQ sauce, not actually placed on the barbecue, instead being baked in the oven. And, if grilled lettuce seems peculiar, don't fret—it's on the grill for a mere minute or so, snuffing out its sweetness and replacing it with a hearty and unique smokiness.

Serves 4

For the Sweet Potato Wedges

2 pounds (about 4 medium) sweet potatoes, cut into wedges lengthwise, measuring ½-inch across

1 tablespoon refined avocado oil or extra-virgin olive oil

½ teaspoon sea salt

For the Sticky BBQ Tempeh

1 (8-ounce) package tempeh, cut into 8 triangles or squares

1 (5.5-ounce) can tomato paste

2 tablespoons apple cider vinegar

1 tablespoon molasses

1 tablespoon vegan, gluten-free Worcestershire sauce

¼ teaspoon garlic powder

¼ teaspoon smoked paprika

¼ teaspoon sea salt

⅛ teaspoon cayenne pepper

For the Grilled Lettuce

2–4 little gem lettuces or small romaine hearts, core intact and halved

For the Ranch Dressing

½ cup canned, full-fat coconut milk

2 scallions, minced

2 teaspoons distilled white vinegar

½ teaspoon dried dill

¼ teaspoon garlic powder

¼ teaspoon sea salt

ground black pepper, to taste

Arrange oven racks in top and bottom thirds of oven. Preheat oven to 425°F.

MAKE AHEAD

Sweet Potato Wedges: 3 days.

Sticky BBQ Tempeh: 3 days.

Ranch Dressing: 3 days.

Make the Sweet Potatoes and Sticky BBQ Tempeh: For the sweet potatoes, on a large-rimmed baking sheet, coat sweet potatoes with oil and salt and spread in a single layer. Roast on top rack for 25 minutes; flip and roast for an additional 10–15 minutes.

For the tempeh, place tempeh in a large casserole dish. In a small bowl, stir together remaining tempeh ingredients; add mixture to tempeh and coat (will seem very thick and gloppy, but use it all). Add to bottom rack of oven in last 20 minutes of roasting sweet potatoes.

Make the Grilled Lettuce: Heat grill or grill pan to medium-high. Add lettuce cut-side down; grill for 30 seconds–1 minute, until grill marks appear. Repeat with remaining lettuce, as necessary.

Make the Ranch Dressing: In a small bowl, combine all dressing ingredients.

To Serve: To bowls, add lettuce, sweet potatoes, and tempeh; top with dressing. Serve.

SOUTH OF THE BORDER BOWLS WITH WALNUT MEAT AND GRILLED AVOCADO

While I'm sure this isn't authentically Mexican, it certainly hits the spot with the trademark, in-your-face flavors. Lime-kissed and surprisingly light, you'll be transported to the warm beaches of Mexico with your first bite. Slather on that SPF, grab your sunglasses, roll up your sleeves, and find a fork—this bowl is for taste bud travelers and flavor cravers.

Serves 4

For the Walnut Meat

2 cups raw walnut halves

2 teaspoons extra-virgin olive oil

1 teaspoon chili powder

1 teaspoon ground cumin

1 teaspoon dried oregano

½ teaspoon sea salt

½ teaspoon smoked mild paprika

¼ teaspoon chili flakes

¼ teaspoon ground cinnamon

For the Grilled Avocado

2 avocados, skin intact and halved

olive oil

For the Lime Sour Cream

1 cup sour cream, preferably full-fat

zest and juice of 1 lime

For Serving

6–8 cups shredded romaine

1 cup cherry tomatoes, halved, or prepared salsa

4 scallions, sliced

MAKE AHEAD

Walnut Meat: 4 days.

Lime Sour Cream: 4 days.

Make the Walnut Meat: In a food processor, pulse all walnut meat ingredients together until it resembles the size of small peas, and the mixture loosely holds together when pressed between two fingers. Do not over-process. Set aside.

Make the Grilled Avocado: Preheat grill or grill pan to medium. Brush avocado flesh with a little oil and place flesh-side down on grill for 5 minutes, or until grill marks appear. Using a large spoon, remove avocado flesh from skin, keeping whole.

Make the Lime Sour Cream: Combine all ingredients in a bowl.

To Serve: To bowls, add a bed of lettuce; top with walnut meat, avocado, sour cream, tomatoes or salsa, and scallions. Serve.

YOGURT PASTA SALAD WITH SUNBLUSH TOMATOES AND ZA'ATAR-MARINATED BUTTER BEANS

A bit of a play on fattoush with pasta in place of pita and composed instead of tossed (however, I love everything tossed together for this, too—it's hard to choose a favorite!). I call these tomatoes "Sunblush" because they're halfway to sundried—still intense in their sweetness but the moisture is kept. For protein and texture, butter beans are doused in za'atar (a Middle Eastern spice blend), a good slick of olive oil, and a smack of lemon. As visually pacifying as it is tasty.

Serves 6

For the Sunblush Tomatoes

2 pints cherry tomatoes, halved

½ teaspoon evaporated cane sugar

½ teaspoon sea salt

For the Za'atar-Marinated Butter Beans

3 cups cooked butter beans

2 tablespoons za'atar (a spice blend containing thyme,

sumac, and sesame seeds), plus additional for serving

2 tablespoons extra-virgin olive oil

2 tablespoons lemon juice

For the Yogurt Pasta Salad

1 pound gluten-free penne or fusilli

¾ cup plain Greek yogurt or Labneh (see page **101**)

1 clove garlic, minced

2 tablespoons extra-virgin olive oil

2 tablespoons lemon juice

sea salt and ground black pepper, to taste

For Serving

6 mini cucumbers or 1 English cucumber, thinly sliced on a bias

> **MAKE AHEAD**
>
> *Yogurt Pasta Salad:* 5 hours.
>
> *Sunblush Tomatoes:* 5 days.
>
> *Za'atar-Marinated Butter Beans:* 5 days.

Make the Sunblush Tomatoes: Preheat oven to 250°F. Line a large-rimmed baking sheet with parchment paper and add tomatoes, skin-side down. Evenly sprinkle sugar and salt over tomatoes. Roast for 2 hours.

Make the Za'atar-Marinated Butter Beans: In a large bowl, combine all marinated bean ingredients. Cover and chill for at last 1 hour.

Make the Yogurt Pasta Salad: Bring a large pot of water to a boil; salt well. Cook pasta according to package directions (8–10 minutes for most brands). Drain, rinse with cold water, and drain again. Add to a large salad bowl.

In a small bowl, combine yogurt, garlic, oil, and lemon juice; season with salt and pepper. Add to pasta and stir to combine.

To Serve: To bowls, add beans, pasta, and cucumber; top with tomatoes and additional za'atar. Or, toss everything together. Serve.

WINTER CHOPPED SALAD

This is a favorite salad recipe from my blog, *Yummy Beet*, containing all of winter's best goodies. The roasted vegetables and fruit alone could be a quick one-tray dinner—just throw on some chickpeas and you're all set.

.... *Serves 4* ....

Salad

1 (2-pound) butternut squash, peeled, seeded, and cut into ½-inch cubes

1 Bosc pear, cored and thinly sliced into strips

1 tablespoon extra-virgin olive oil

¼ teaspoon sea salt

1 pound green beans, chopped into ½-inch pieces

5 ounces (6–8 cups) arugula

1 cup cubed feta cheese

¼ cup hulled sunflower seeds

Dressing

2 tablespoons roasted hazelnut oil or extra-virgin olive oil

2 tablespoons lemon juice

1 clove garlic, minced

2 teaspoons Dijon mustard

1 teaspoon dried thyme

½ teaspoon sea salt

MAKE AHEAD

Roasted Vegetables: 3 days.

Dressing: 3 days.

Make the roasted vegetables: Preheat oven to 400°F. On a large-rimmed baking sheet, toss squash and pear with oil and salt. Roast for 25 minutes. Add green beans, stir to incorporate, and roast for an additional 10 minutes.

Make the Dressing: In a small jar (to shake) or small bowl (to whisk), combine all dressing ingredients.

To Serve: In a large salad bowl, toss all salad components and dressing. Serve.

BLACK RICE AND BROCCOLI RABE SALAD WITH APRICOTS AND PINE NUTS

This salad can be eaten warm, room temperature, or chilled, making it a bit of a seasonless recipe. Don't be afraid to gild the lily with a poached egg, crumbling of feta, or dollop of hummus—I know I'm certainly not.

Serves 4–6

For the Salad
⅔ cup black rice
1⅓ cups water
1 bunch broccoli rabe (rapini), cut into bite-sized pieces

10 dried apricots, sliced
1 tablespoon extra-virgin olive oil
1 tablespoon balsamic vinegar
¾ teaspoon sea salt

ground black pepper, to taste
⅛ teaspoon grated nutmeg
2 tablespoons pine nuts

MAKE AHEAD

Salad (dressed):
2 days.

Make the black rice: In a medium saucepan, bring rice and water to a boil, reduce to a simmer, cover, and cook for 45 minutes. Turn off heat and steam, covered, for 5 minutes.

Make the Salad: Bring a large pot of water to a boil. Blanch rapini for 1–2 minutes. Drain and run very cold tap water over to halt cooking. Drain again and gently press to remove excess liquid. Give another chop if pieces are too big. Add back to pot along with cooked rice, apricots, oil, vinegar, salt, pepper, and nutmeg. Toast pine nuts over medium in a skillet, being careful not to burn (only takes 45 seconds or so); mix into salad.

To Serve: Divide amongst bowls. Serve warm, room temperature, or chilled.

KALE CAESAR SALAD WITH SMOKY SWEET POTATOES AND QUINOA PUMPKIN SEED CROUTONS

This take on the classic Caesar salad is the kind of meal where, after you're finished, you stick your finger in the bowl and swirl around for one last taste when no one's looking. Unlike the traditional version calling for romaine lettuce, kale is belle of the ball here. There are a couple of benefits to this, namely, the kale's taste and texture improve once dressed, allowing you to make this a couple days in advance. Sweet potatoes hit with smoked paprika add that stock, smoky bacon taste. And croutons. I haven't forgotten about the croutons!

.... *Serves 4* ....

For the Quinoa Pumpkin Seed Croutons

¾ cup water

½ cup uncooked quinoa

½ cup finely grated pecorino romano or parmesan cheese

¼ cup raw pumpkin seeds

1 teaspoon dried thyme

For the Smoky Sweet Potatoes

1½ pounds (about 2 medium) sweet potatoes, cut into ½-inch cubes

1 tablespoon extra-virgin olive oil

1 teaspoon mild smoked paprika

½ teaspoon sea salt

For the Dressing

½ cup mayonnaise (see page **198**)

2 tablespoons lemon juice

1 tablespoon Dijon mustard

1 tablespoon vegan, gluten-free Worcestershire sauce

1 clove garlic, minced

ground black pepper, to taste (I like a lot in this dressing)

For Serving

½ bunch (4–5 cups) kale destemmed and torn into bite-sized pieces

MAKE AHEAD

Salad: 2 days.

Smoky Sweet Potatoes: 5 days.

Quinoa Pumpkin Seed Croutons: 1 week.

Caesar Dressing: 1 week.

Arrange oven racks in the top and middle sections of oven. Preheat oven to 400°F.

Make the Quinoa Pumpkin Seed Croutons and Smoky Sweet Potatoes: Line a large-rimmed baking sheet with parchment paper. For croutons, add water and quinoa to a medium saucepan; bring to a boil, reduce to a simmer, cover, and cook for 15 minutes. Remove from heat, uncover, and cool for 10 minutes (so cheese doesn't melt). Stir in cheese, seeds, and thyme. Press into a ¼-inch thick layer onto prepared baking sheet to make one large "cookie."

For sweet potatoes, on a separate large-rimmed baking sheet (no parchment required), toss all sweet potato ingredients together.

Add croutons to top rack of oven and sweet potatoes to bottom rack. Roast for 30 minutes. Toss sweet potatoes (if croutons look brown enough, remove now). Roast for an additional 5–10 minutes. Remove croutons; cool (croutons will crisp as they cool) on baking sheet completely. If not using immediately, break croutons into pieces and store in an airtight container in the pantry.

Make the Caesar Dressing: Mix all dressing ingredients together in a small bowl.

To Serve: In a large salad bowl, massage kale with your hands until bright green; break over shards of crouton. Add sweet potatoes and dressing; toss to combine. Serve.

NOTES

Unlike romaine lettuce that goes limp when dressed, the longer the kale gets to marinate in the dressing, the better this bowl becomes.

RAINBOW VEGETABLE SLAW WITH PISTACHIOS AND HARISSA DRESSING

Like traditional salads, slaws can vary. This particular slaw errs on the lighter side, taking a cue from Morocco in terms of its flavor profile. To garnish, thick, steak-like rounds of orange are the meat of the dish; pistachios lend a hand in terms richness and eye-popping color; and cool yogurt keeps the harissa's heat levels in check.

.... *Serves 6* ....

For the Harissa Dressing
⅓ cup extra-virgin olive oil
¼ cup lemon juice
1 tablespoon red wine vinegar
2 tablespoons harissa paste (see page **197**)
½ teaspoon sea salt, more to taste

For the Slaw
½ small head (4–5 cups shredded) red cabbage, finely shredded
2 cups (about 2) grated carrots
1 cup (about 2) grated beets
1 cup fresh mint or cilantro, roughly chopped

2 cups cooked chickpeas
6 navel oranges, peeled and cut crosswise into ½-inch rounds
1 cup plain Greek yogurt
½ cup raw, shelled, unsalted pistachios, roughly chopped

MAKE AHEAD

Slaw: 4 days. Garnish with oranges, yogurt, and pistachios just before serving.

Harissa Dressing: 1 week.

NOTES

If you have a food processor, take advantage of its shredding/grating attachment for a lightning-fast slaw.

Make the Harissa Dressing: In a small bowl, whisk all dressing ingredients until combined. Cover and refrigerate until ready to serve.

Make the Slaw: In a large salad bowl, toss cabbage, carrots, beets, mint or cilantro, and chickpeas; add dressing and mix to coat. Taste, seasoning with additional salt if necessary. Cover and chill for 1 hour or longer to marinate, if desired (recommended).

To Serve: Divide amongst bowls; top with a fan of orange slices, dollop of yogurt, and sprinkle of pistachios. Serve.

SPRING SMASHED CHICKPEA SALAD WITH CURRY MAYO

Smashed chickpeas, crunchy celery, pretty peas, and a sunlit curry mayo combine in a flash for a legume-based variation of the traditional egg or chicken salads. A hefty serving of this on top of a bed of spring greens is all that's required to make it come to life. However, if you want to think outside of the bowl, this salad is wonderful in a wrap or sandwiched with a fat slice of tomato between toasted seed bread.

Serves 4

For the Curry Mayo

½ cup mayonnaise (see page **198**)

1 clove garlic, minced

2 tablespoons lemon juice

2 teaspoons curry powder

½ teaspoon sea salt

For the Spring Smashed Chickpea Salad

3 cups cooked chickpeas

1½ cups diced celery

1 cup fresh or frozen, defrosted green peas

½ cup sliced fresh basil

2 tablespoons dried currants or raisins

For Serving

8 cups spring mix lettuce

lemon juice or balsamic vinegar

sea salt, to taste

¼ cup sunflower seeds

MAKE AHEAD

Spring Smashed Chickpea Salad: 4 days.

Curry Mayo: 1 week.

Make the Curry Mayo: In a small bowl, combine all mayo ingredients.

Make the Spring Smashed Chickpea Salad: In a large bowl, roughly smash chickpeas with a pastry cutter or fork, leaving plenty of texture. Add remaining salad ingredients and mayo; mix well to incorporate.

To Serve: In a large bowl, toss lettuce with lemon juice or balsamic vinegar; season with salt. To bowls, add a bed of lettuce; top with chickpea salad and sunflower seeds. Serve.

TUNISIAN PARSLEY SALAD WITH KABOCHA SQUASH, DUKKAH, AND SPICED YOGURT

The countries of North Africa contribute the panoply of assertive components in this big-bowl salad. Lettuce is replaced with the chlorophyll-rich herb parsley for a palate-pleasing salad swap. Dried fruit adds a sweet, caramel-like surprise as you work your way through this bowl, foiling the bitter radicchio and spicy dressing. And, if you're looking to gild the lily, briny black olives find themselves at home here quite well.

Serves 4–6, with extra Spiced Yogurt

For the Salad

- 1 (2-pound) kabocha or red kuri squash, peeled, seeded, and cut into ½-inch cubes
- 1 tablespoon extra-virgin olive oil
- ¼ teaspoon sea salt
- 1 head radicchio, roughly chopped
- 1 bunch (⅓ pound) flat leaf parsley, tough stems removed, leaves separated
- ¼ cup diced medjool dates or dried currants
- ¼ cup Hazelnut Dukkah (see page **39**)

For the Spiced Yogurt

- 1 cup whole milk plain yogurt
- ⅓ cup tahini
- 3 tablespoons lemon juice
- 1 heaping tablespoon harissa paste (see page **197**)
- 1 teaspoon sea salt

MAKE AHEAD

Roasted Squash: 3 days.

Salad (dressed): 3 days.

Spiced Yogurt: 1 week.

NOTES

Use leftover Spiced Yogurt as a dip for sweet potato wedges, a dressing for romaine lettuce, a veggie burger condiment, or anywhere else that needs something creamy, bright, and a touch spicy.

Make the roasted squash: Preheat oven to 400°F. On a large-rimmed baking sheet, combine squash, oil, and salt. Roast for 35–40 minutes, until tender.

Make the Spiced Yogurt: In a medium bowl, whisk all yogurt ingredients until fully incorporated.

To Serve: In a large salad bowl, toss roasted squash, remaining salad ingredients, and ½ of the yogurt (or add enough until it looks right to you). Serve and keep dressing handy to add more at the table.

ALMOND NOODLE SALAD WITH RADISHES AND BASIL

This is my blatantly North American interpretation of a cuisine—a potpourri of international tastes, if you will. A nod to Thai cuisine, floral basil is the greenery. Japan's contributions are tamari and wasabi imbued radishes that practically dance on the palate with their earthquaking crunch. And China and South India provide the sesame elements. All these ingredients get along famously for a healthier take-out facsimile that's, at the very least, authentically tasty.

Serves 4–6

For the Noodle Salad

1 pound gluten-free brown rice spaghetti or gluten-free brown rice linguini

1 (7-ounce) package smoked tofu, drained and cut into ½-inch cubes

1 bunch (½ pound) radishes, greens removed and quartered

1 carrot, shaved with a julienne peeler or grated

1 red bell pepper, seeded and sliced into thin strips

1 cup sliced fresh basil, plus more to garnish

2 tablespoons white or black sesame seeds

1 tablespoon toasted sesame oil

For the Almond Sauce

⅓ cup unsalted natural almond butter (smooth or crunchy)

3 tablespoons tamari

2 tablespoons unseasoned rice vinegar

1 tablespoon white miso

1 tablespoon toasted sesame oil

1 tablespoon grated fresh ginger

1 clove garlic, minced

Water, as needed

MAKE AHEAD

Noodle Salad: 4 days.

Almond Sauce: 2 weeks.

Make the Noodle Salad: Bring a large pot of water to a boil; salt well. Cook pasta according to package directions, drain, rinse well with cold water, and drain again. Add pasta to a large salad bowl along with remaining salad ingredients and toss to combine.

Make the Almond Sauce: In a medium bowl, whisk all sauce ingredients together. Thin with water, 1 tablespoon at a time until desired consistency (you may need up to 4 tablespoons).

To Serve: To bowls, add salad, making sure to get plenty of vegetables and tofu in each serving. Drizzle with sauce and sprinkle with additional basil. Serve.

THREE-BEAN GARDEN SALAD WITH ASPARAGUS AND COCONUT DRESSING

My mom was an expert gardener, and try as I might, I'm personally a bit clumsy in this area. Each year I make promises to myself and do manage to come out with a few edibles, but really shouldn't quit my day job, if you know what I mean. Whether you grow and harvest the vegetables for this salad yourself, the flavors in this gorgeously green bowl do all the heavy lifting and tilling to cultivate a freshly picked garden taste. (Bonus: no dirty fingernails or back spasms).

Serves 5–6

For the Salad

½ pound green beans, tough ends removed, cut into 1-inch pieces on a bias

½ pound wax (yellow) beans, tough ends removed, cut into 1-inch pieces on a bias

1 pound green or white asparagus, tough ends removed, cut into 1-inch pieces on a bias

2 cups cooked butter beans

½ cup fresh or frozen, defrosted green peas

½ cup roasted hazelnuts, roughly chopped (see page **206**)

For the Coconut Dressing

1 cup coconut milk (thick, canned)

2 cloves garlic, minced

6 tablespoons lime juice

2 tablespoons extra-virgin olive oil

2–3 teaspoons sea salt

ground black pepper, to taste

> **MAKE AHEAD**
>
> *Salad (dressed):* 3 days.
>
> *Coconut Dressing:* 1 week.

Make the Salad: Steam green and wax beans until tender-crisp (3–5 minutes). Immediately run cold tap water over beans to preserve color and cool down. Steam asparagus according to bean directions. Dry as much water off steamed beans and asparagus as possible with a clean dish or paper towel.

Make the Dressing: In a small bowl, combine all dressing ingredients.

To Serve: In a large salad bowl, toss all salad ingredients with desired amount of dressing (you may have extra). Serve.

SMOKY CORN AND GRILLED PEACH SALAD WITH BLACK BEANS AND CILANTRO JALAPEÑO PESTO

It's just so easy to become captivated by summer produce in all of its piñata painted splendor. Bumblebee confetti of corn and black beans, along with beady quinoa, act as a bank for big, fat, grilled-to-perfection peaches. It all gets super soakered with a verdant pesto that hits you at the back of your throat with jalapeño's trademark bite-back.

Serves 4

For the Cilantro Jalapeño Pesto

1 clove garlic

1 jalapeño, seeds removed and roughly chopped

¼ cup raw or roasted almonds

½ bunch fresh cilantro, stems included

¼ cup extra-virgin olive oil

2 tablespoons white wine vinegar

1 teaspoon sea salt

For the Smoky Corn

1 tablespoon refined avocado oil or extra-virgin olive oil

2 cups fresh or frozen (defrosted) corn kernels

½ teaspoon smoked paprika

½ teaspoon sea salt

ground black pepper, to taste

For the Bowls

2 peaches, halved and pitted

refined avocado oil or extra-virgin olive oil

2 cups cooked black beans

2 cups cooked quinoa (see page **209**)

MAKE AHEAD

Smoky Corn: 2 days.

Grilled Peaches: 2 days.

Cilantro Jalapeño Pesto: 4 days.

Make the Cilantro Jalapeño Pesto: In a food processor, pulse garlic and jalapeño until minced, add almonds and cilantro, and pulse again until minced. Add oil, vinegar, and salt; blend until desired smoothness.

Make the Smoky Corn: Heat oil in a large sauté pan over medium. Add corn, paprika, salt, and pepper; sauté for 5–8 minutes.

Make the Grilled Peaches: Preheat grill pan or grill to medium. Rub a little oil on peach flesh. Add peach halves, flesh-side down to grill pan or grill; cook for 5–8 minutes, or until grill marks appear.

To Serve: In a medium bowl, toss black beans with ⅓ of the pesto. To serving bowls, add corn, beans, and quinoa; top with a grilled peach half and remaining pesto. Serve.

MOROCCAN NIÇOISE WITH LABNEH AND GOLDEN MILLET

Having been to Nice, France, I can assure you I made it a priority to eat a "real" Salade Niçoise. Well, good news: as long as the ingredients are fresh, the North American versions are practically indistinguishable from the "real" ones (less the rosé and bread accompanying the meal—France wins by a long shot in that regard). They're one of the original bowls thanks to their artful composition, and here, I've melded countries and flavors for a nouveau take on the lunchtime classic.

Serves 4

For the Labneh
1 cup whole milk or 2% plain yogurt

For the Golden Millet
1 cup water
½ cup millet
1 teaspoon turmeric
¼ teaspoon saffron
¼ teaspoon sea salt

1 cup roughly chopped cilantro, tender stems included
3 scallions, sliced
¼ cup raisins
¼ cup roasted almonds, chopped

For the Salad
1 head green leaf lettuce, torn
4 hardboiled eggs, peeled and halved

1½ cups cherry tomatoes, halved
4 mini cucumbers, cut on a bias into ¼-inch slices
½ cup dry-cured black olives or Niçoise olives, pitted
extra-virgin olive oil
lemon juice
za'atar

MAKE AHEAD

Golden Millet: 3 days.

Labneh: 2 weeks.

Make the Labneh: Line a colander with cheesecloth (or clean cloth, or coffee filter) and place over a bowl, making sure bottom of colander doesn't touch bottom of bowl. Add yogurt to lined colander and refrigerate for at least 5 hours, until water collects at bottom and yogurt is very thick. Discard water (or use in smoothies).

Make the Golden Millet: In a medium saucepan, combine water, millet, turmeric, saffron, and salt. Bring to a boil, reduce to a simmer, cover, and cook for 20 minutes. Remove from heat and steam, covered, for 5 minutes. Transfer to a large bowl along with remaining millet ingredients and toss to combine.

To Serve: To bowls, add a bed of lettuce; top with compartments of labneh, millet, eggs, tomatoes, cucumbers, and olives. Season with oil, lemon juice, and za'atar. Serve.

Chapter 3: Entrée Whole Bowls

This chapter was the jumping off point for the entire *Whole Bowls* cookbook. It's filled with meal-in-a-bowl feasts that take the guesswork out of healthy, plant-based eating, borrowing inspiration from all corners of the world. These are vegetable-focused and wholly satisfying dishes that vegetarians, vegans, omnivores, and gluten-free diners can all enjoy at the same table. Here, you'll find recipes for spice lovers, Mexican food fanatics, grilling gurus, and take-out queens and kings.

These entrées are focused on whole grains, fresh produce, zippy condiments, and plant-based proteins that will satisfy any time constraint or penchant. Like the preceding chapters, I've included Make Ahead notes on many of the pages (when applicable), allowing you to prep, cook, save, and eat well during a chaotic weekly schedule. There are recipes to languish over, ones to whip up in a pinch, stews to stir, and bowls that wow.

For the inveterate kitchen dalliers (me), the hasty I-need-to-eat-right-this-moment-or-I'll-parish crowd, and those who have but one day a week to even think about cooking a meal, I assure you, there's a recipe in the following pages for you. Make a little now, save a little for later, or whip it up all at once, whatever you do, enter this chapter with a healthy appetite, a sharp knife, and a handful of greens.

ENTRÉE WHOLE BOWLS

SPRING RICE BOWLS WITH CHIVE OIL
109

BOHEMIAN BOWLS WITH CHILI SQUASH AND TAHINI DRESSING
111

BANQUET BOWLS WITH CAULIFLOWER HAZELNUT PILAF,
DHAL, AND SCALLION CUCUMBER RAITA
113

FOREST BOWLS WITH WILD RICE, MUSHROOMS, AND ROASTED
GARLIC COCONUT GRAVY
115

HOLIDAY BOWLS WITH STUFFING, SWEET POTATO LATKES,
BRUSSELS SPROUTS, AND BALSAMIC GLAZE
117

VEGAN PHO WITH DELICATA SQUASH AND ENOKI MUSHROOMS
121

EVERYDAY BOWLS WITH APPLE DRESSING AND FETA
122

GREEK MUSHROOM STIFADO WITH HORSERADISH
MASHED POTATOES
125

MISO MEAL IN A BOWL
127

PURPLE VEGETABLE RICE BOWL
128

BLACK BEANS WITH BUTTERNUT SQUASH, BLACK RICE,
AND CHIMICHURRI
131

SPRING RICE BOWLS WITH CHIVE OIL

Lush, fat, healthy greens that poke their heads up in early April and May are worthy of a little celebration. Vibrant and light, this bowl is a refreshingly simple way to recalibrate the palate after a winter of heartier repasts.

Serves 4

For the Bowls

1 cup uncooked short grain brown rice

2 cups water

1 pound asparagus, tough ends trimmed, cut into 1-inch pieces (leave some water clinging)

2 cups cooked chickpeas

¾ cup fresh or dry, cooked and peeled, or frozen, defrosted fava beans

2 carrots, julienned, shaved, or shredded

For the Chive Oil

3 tablespoons extra-virgin olive oil

1 tablespoon lemon juice

1 tablespoon finely diced fresh chives, plus chive blossoms for garnish (optional)

½ teaspoons sea salt

ground black pepper, to taste

MAKE AHEAD

Assembled Bowls: 2 days.

Brown Rice: 3 days.

Make the Bowls: Preheat oven to 400°F. For the brown rice, in a medium saucepan, bring water and rice to a boil, reduce to a simmer, cover, and cook for 45 minutes. Steam, covered for 5 minutes; fluff with fork before serving.

For the asparagus, add to a large-rimmed baking sheet. Roast in preheated oven for 10 minutes. Alternatively, steam asparagus for 3–5 minutes.

In a medium bowl, combine chickpeas with fava beans.

Make the Chive Oil: In a small bowl, combine all chive oil ingredients.

To Serve: To bowls, arrange brown rice, chickpeas and fava beans, asparagus, and carrot. Drizzle with chive oil and garnish with chive blossoms (if using). Serve warm or chilled.

BOHEMIAN BOWLS WITH CHILI SQUASH AND TAHINI DRESSING

Don't be turned off by the whimsical (somewhat leftist) title—there's no card-carrying granola status required, only a good appetite. Simple in its preparation, the grains, broccoli, and chickpeas are kept neutral, allowing the punchy dressing to steal the spotlight. Combined with sunset-stained, chili-spiked squash, this bowl will make you want to hippie hippie shake! Embrace your inner treehugger and chow down on this new classic, euphoric bowl.

Serves 4, with leftover Tahini Dressing

For the Chili Squash

1 (2-pound) kabocha or red kuri squash, seeded and cut into 8 wedges, or peeled and cubed into ½-inch pieces

1 tablespoon coconut oil or extra-virgin olive oil

2 teaspoons coconut sugar or evaporated cane sugar

½ teaspoon chili flakes

½ teaspoon sea salt

For the Tahini Dressing (makes 1½ cups)

½ cup room temperature water, plus additional to thin, as required

½ cup tahini

¼ cup lemon juice

1 clove garlic, finely minced

2 tablespoons nutritional yeast

1 tablespoon tamari

¼ teaspoon ground black pepper

Steamed Beans and Broccoli

2 cups cooked chickpeas

1 head broccoli, cut into florets

For Serving

2 cups hot, cooked grain of choice (see page **209**)

sprouts (alfalfa, pea, sunflower, radish, etc.)

MAKE AHEAD

Steamed Beans and Broccoli: 3 days.

Chili Squash: 4 days.

Tahini Dressing: 7 days.

Make the Chili Squash: Preheat oven to 400°F. Line a large-rimmed baking sheet with parchment paper. Add wedges (skin-side down) or cubes; rub oil over wedges or toss cubes with oil. Sprinkle evenly with sugar, chili, and salt; rub over wedges or toss to coat cubes. Roast for 30–35 minutes, until tender.

Make the Tahini Dressing: Add all dressing ingredients to a blender or food processor or medium bowl; blend or whisk by hand until smooth and slightly whipped. Add water, 1 tablespoon at a time, if a thinner dressing is desired.

Make the Steamed Beans and Broccoli: Add chickpeas and broccoli to a steamer basket. Steam until broccoli is tender and beans are heated through (3–5 minutes).

To Serve: To bowls, arrange beans and broccoli, grains, and squash; top with dressing and sprouts. Serve.

BANQUET BOWLS WITH CAULIFLOWER HAZELNUT PILAF, DHAL, AND SCALLION CUCUMBER RAITA

The components of this very special bowl will fill your home with the heady aroma of basmati rice, daffodil-dyed curry, rich coconut, and cooling cucumber. It's worth the laundry list of ingredients typical of a well-rounded curry banquet.

Serves 5–6

For the Cauliflower Hazelnut Pilaf

2 tablespoons coconut oil

1 onion, diced

2 cloves garlic, minced

1 tablespoon fresh grated ginger

1 tablespoon curry powder (mild or hot)

2 teaspoons garam masala

1 teaspoon sea salt

ground black pepper, to taste

1 cup brown basmati rice, rinsed well and drained

1¾ cups water

1 tablespoon lemon juice

1 small head or ½ large head cauliflower, chopped into very tiny pieces

½ cup roasted hazelnuts, chopped (see page **206**)

½ cup chopped fresh cilantro

For the Dhal

3½ cups water

2 cups dry red lentils

½ cup coconut milk

2 teaspoons lemon juice

2 teaspoons maple syrup

2 teaspoons curry powder (mild or hot)

1 teaspoon sea salt

For the Scallion Cucumber Raita

1 cup diced English cucumber

¾ cup plain Greek yogurt

¼ cup cilantro, chopped

4 scallions, sliced

1 teaspoon lemon juice

MAKE AHEAD

Cauliflower Hazelnut Pilaf: 2 days.

Scallion Cucumber Raita: 3 days.

Dhal: 1 week.

Make the Cauliflower Hazelnut Pilaf: In a large pot (do not use a high-sided skillet or rice will not cook properly), heat oil over medium. Add onion, garlic, ginger, spices, salt, and pepper. Sauté for 10 minutes, until onions are soft. Add rice, stirring constantly to toast for 2 minutes, followed by water and lemon juice. Bring to a boil, reduce to a simmer, cover, and cook for 45 minutes. Stir in cauliflower, cover, increase heat slightly, and cook for an additional 10 minutes, or until cauliflower is tender. Remove from heat and fold in hazelnuts and cilantro.

Make the Dhal: Place all ingredients for dhal in a large high-sided skillet or medium saucepan. Bring to a boil, reduce to a simmer, and cook, uncovered for 20–25 minutes, stirring often.

Make the Scallion Cucumber Raita: In a medium bowl, mix all raita ingredients together until incorporated.

To Serve: To bowls, fill one side with pilaf, followed by dhal opposite, and generously dollop raita in a corner. (It tastes wonderful as it mixes in.) Serve.

FOREST BOWLS WITH WILD RICE, MUSHROOMS, AND ROASTED GARLIC COCONUT GRAVY

This bowl was inspired by my trip to Tofino, British Columbia, Canada, where I spent many hours hiking around the famous, larger-than-life redwoods. Like a good trail blaze, there's something especially therapeutic about eating a bowl of earth tones. Spiky wild rice is the base for earthy mushrooms, irony greens, beans, and coconut gravy smoothed out with sweet roasted garlic. Don't be afraid of using an entire head of garlic—once roasted, its sharpness disappears, lending only a quiet garlicky note to the gravy (and no vampire-spooking breath afterward). This forager's feast is a treat for the senses.

·· *Serves 4* ··

For the Roasted Garlic Coconut Gravy

1 head garlic, halved crosswise

½ cup water

2 tablespoons arrowroot flour

1 (14-ounce) can full-fat coconut milk

1 tablespoon extra-virgin olive oil

2 teaspoons apple cider vinegar

1 teaspoon sea salt

½ teaspoon dried thyme

¼ teaspoon ground black pepper

pinch, ground nutmeg

For the Wild Rice

3 cups water

1 cup uncooked wild rice

¼ teaspoon sea salt

¼ cup raisins or chopped dried cranberries

For the Mushrooms, Greens, and Beans

1 tablespoon extra-virgin olive oil

¾ pound (4 cups, sliced) cremini, shiitake (stemmed), or button mushrooms (or a mixture), sliced

1 teaspoon sea salt

2 cups cooked chickpeas

½ bunch (4–5 cups) kale, de-stemmed and torn into bite-sized pieces

MAKE AHEAD

Mushrooms, Greens, and Beans: 2 days.

Roasted Garlic Coconut Gravy: 4 days; 2 months, frozen.

Wild Rice: 4 days.

Make the Roasted Garlic Coconut Gravy: Preheat oven to 400°F. Crunch up garlic into a ball in foil. Roast for 45 minutes. Carefully open foil to cool for 15 minutes. In a small bowl, whisk water with arrowroot. Once the garlic is cool enough to handle, squeeze the cloves (discard papery skin) into a medium saucepan or skillet, along with arrowroot mixture and remaining gravy ingredients; whisk until mixed. Over medium heat, whisking constantly, bring to a boil, reduce to a simmer, and cook for 1–2 minutes. Immediately before serving, warm gravy over medium-low heat, whisking constantly.

Make the Wild Rice: In a medium saucepan, bring water, rice, and salt to a boil. Reduce to a simmer, cover, and cook for 45–50 minutes; test for doneness (grains should be burst).

(Continued on page 116)

Drain rice in a sieve, return to pot, and stir in raisins or cranberries. Cover and keep warm.

Make the Mushrooms, Greens, and Beans: In a large high-sided skillet, heat oil over medium heat. Add mushrooms and salt; sauté until tender (5–8 minutes). Add chickpeas and kale; briefly cook until chickpeas are heated through and kale is wilted (add a splash of water to help the process along if needed).

To Serve: To bowls, add a bed of rice; top with mushrooms, greens, and beans. Generously ladle warm gravy over. Serve.

HOLIDAY BOWLS WITH STUFFING, SWEET POTATO LATKES, BRUSSELS SPROUTS, AND BALSAMIC GLAZE

Often, it's the appetizers, snacks, and sides of holiday feasts that steal the show, so I've included some of my favorite seasonal flavors for one big soiree in a bowl. At the end, it's Jackson Pollocked with sticky balsamic glaze, making this entrée practically twinkle like tree lights.

.... *Serves 4* ....

For the Stuffing

¾ cup uncooked brown lentils

¾ cup water (for quinoa)

½ cup uncooked quinoa

4 scallions, sliced

2 small apples, cored and cut into small cubes

¼ cup dried cranberries, chopped

1 tablespoon lemon juice

1 teaspoon sea salt

1 teaspoon dried thyme

1 teaspoon coconut oil or butter

For the Latkes (makes 8–10)

2 tablespoons refined avocado oil or extra-virgin olive oil

1 large egg

2 teaspoons dried chopped onion

1 teaspoon sea salt

ground black pepper, to taste

1 pound (about 1 large) sweet potatoes, grated

¾ pound (about 2) Yukon Gold potatoes, grated and squeezed to remove excess water

2 tablespoons coconut flour

For the Brussels Sprouts

1 pound Brussels sprouts, halved

1 tablespoon extra-virgin olive oil

½ teaspoon sea salt

For Serving

Balsamic Glaze (see page **197**)

MAKE AHEAD

Brussels Sprouts: 3 days.

Stuffing: 5 days.

Sweet Potato Latkes: 5 days. Reheat in a 400°F oven for 10 minutes, or until hot and crisp.

Arrange oven racks in top and bottom thirds of oven to accommodate two trays. Preheat oven to 425°F.

Make the Stuffing: In a large pot, add lentils and cover with 2 inches of water. Bring to a boil, reduce to medium, and cook for 20–25 minutes until tender. Drain, rinse, and add back to pot. Meanwhile, in a medium saucepan, bring ¾ cup water and quinoa to a boil, reduce to a simmer, cover, and cook for 15 minutes. Remove from heat and steam, covered for 5 minutes. Add cooked quinoa to lentils, along with remaining stuffing ingredients. Stir to combine and reheat over low for a few minutes before serving.

(Continued on page 118)

Make the Latkes and Brussels Sprouts: For the latkes, line a large-rimmed baking sheet with parchment paper; grease paper with oil. In a large bowl, beat egg with dried onion, salt, and pepper. Add grated potatoes, mixing well, followed by coconut flour, and mix again (using hands to mix is best) until combined. Scoop scant ½ cup-sized amounts of latke mixture onto oiled parchment, pressing down firmly to ½-inch high (you want them very compact, shaped like a burger). Bake for 30 minutes on top rack. Carefully flip and press down with spatula to compact them further. Bake for 10 to 15 minutes longer (add Brussels sprouts to oven at this point; see below).

For the Brussels sprouts, on a separate large-rimmed baking sheet, toss Brussels sprouts with oil and salt. Roast on bottom rack for 10–15 minutes, until brown and tender.

To Serve: To bowls, add a side of stuffing, a fan of latkes, and a scoop of Brussels sprouts. Drizzle with balsamic glaze. Serve.

VEGAN PHO WITH DELICATA SQUASH AND ENOKI MUSHROOMS

A restorative, traditional Vietnamese soup with a vegan twist, this aromatic pho will leave you feeling perfectly revitalized. And while it may look involved, it could be easier to put together. If you're not concerned with presentation, there's no need to be fussy in the ingredient placement as I've directed—it's a tie your hair back, slurp, and savor kind of meal anyways.

Serves 2

For the Squash

1 delicata squash (sweet potato squash), halved lengthwise, seeded, cut crosswise into ¼-inch half rounds

1 tablespoon extra-virgin olive oil or refined avocado oil

For the Pho Broth

3 cups water

2 cloves garlic, minced

2 tablespoons brown rice miso or mellow white miso

1 tablespoon maple syrup

1 tablespoon unseasoned rice vinegar

1 tablespoon tamari

1-inch piece ginger, peeled, left whole

2 whole star anise

1 cinnamon stick

¼ teaspoon chili flakes

2½ ounces enoki mushrooms, separated

For Serving

4 ounces gluten-free brown rice spaghetti or whole grain spaghetti of choice, cooked, drained, rinsed with cold water, drained again, room temperature

½ block (4–6 ounces) extra-firm tofu, pressed if you have time, cut into matchsticks or cubed, room temperature

1 cup fresh basil leaves

1 teaspoon sesame seeds

> **MAKE AHEAD**
>
> *Broth:* 1 week.
>
> *Roasted Delicata Squash:* 3 days.

Make the Squash: Preheat oven to 400°F. Line a large-rimmed baking sheet with parchment paper, add squash, and toss with oil. Roast for 20–25 minutes, until tender. While squash is roasting, prepare the broth.

Make the Broth: In a large saucepan, slowly whisk water into garlic, miso, maple syrup, vinegar, and tamari. Mix in ginger, star anise, cinnamon, chili, and mushrooms. Bring to a gentle simmer over medium-high, cover, reduce to low, and simmer for 20 minutes. Discard ginger, star anise, and cinnamon stick.

To Serve: Ladle hot broth (including mushrooms) into very large, deep bowls. Top with sections of noodles, roasted squash, tofu, and basil. Sprinkle with sesame seeds and serve.

EVERYDAY BOWLS WITH APPLE DRESSING AND FETA

Chockfull of seasonless, familiar, and healthful ingredients, this bowl is idyllic for those off-peak times when nothing seems to look overly fresh at the markets, and even better when the vegetables are at their peak. With a couple of hardworking pantry proteins—chickpeas and quinoa—along with a sweet and sour apple dressing, these bowls are an everyday dinner solution.

Serves 4

Apple Dressing

½ cup apple juice or apple cider (not vinegar)

3 tablespoons extra-virgin olive oil

2 tablespoons apple cider vinegar

1 teaspoon whole grain mustard

1 teaspoon Dijon mustard

¼ teaspoon sea salt

For the One-Tray Vegetables

1 pound (about 2 medium) sweet potatoes, cut into ½-inch chunks

1 pound (about 4 small) beets, cut into ½-inch chunks

1 tablespoon fresh chopped or dried rosemary

½ teaspoon sea salt

ground black pepper, to taste

3 tablespoons Apple Dressing (recipe above)

½ bunch (4–5 cups) kale, de-stemmed, torn into bite-sized pieces

For the Quinoa and Chickpeas

1 cup water

½ cup uncooked quinoa

2 cups cooked chickpeas

For Serving

4 ounces feta cheese, sliced crosswise into ½-inch strips (about the size of a domino)

Preheat oven to 400°F.

Make the Dressing: In a small saucepan, bring apple juice or cider to a boil, reduce heat to medium, allowing to rapidly simmer for 8–10 minutes until reduced by half to make ¼ cup. Transfer to a small bowl (or glass jar to shake), whisk in remaining ingredients until emulsified.

Make the One-Tray Vegetables: On a large-rimmed baking sheet, toss sweet potatoes, beets, rosemary, salt, pepper, and 3 tablespoons Apple Dressing together. Roast for 25 minutes, toss, and roast for an additional 20 minutes, adding the kale directly on top in the last 5 minutes of cooking, until wilted. Toss to combine all vegetables.

Make the Quinoa and Chickpeas: In a medium saucepan, bring water and quinoa to a boil, reduce to a simmer, cover, and cook for 15 minutes. Keeping heat low, add chickpeas on top, cover, and steam for 5 minutes until heated through. Toss to combine before serving.

To Serve: To bowls, add a bed of quinoa and chickpeas; top vegetables, feta, and remaining dressing. Serve.

> **MAKE AHEAD**
>
> *One-Tray Vegetables:* 3 days.
>
> *Quinoa and Chickpeas:* 3 days.
>
> *Apple Dressing:* 1 week.

GREEK MUSHROOM STIFADO WITH HORSERADISH MASHED POTATOES

Opulent, decadent, delicious, warming—these are just a few of the words that come to mind when eating this. You can make this traditional Greek meal in a bowl any time of year; however, I developed and tested this recipe on several bitterly cold Canadian winter evenings. Every time, my house was perfumed with the most spectacular comfort food aroma, making me sit and count down the moments until dinner for the taste test.

.... *Serves 4* ....

For the Mushroom Stifado

2 tablespoons unsalted butter

1½ pounds (5–6 cups, quartered) mixed mushrooms (a cremini and button mix is great)

2 onions, quartered

4 cloves garlic, minced

2 teaspoons sea salt

2 teaspoons fresh chopped or dried rosemary

2 bay leaves

1 teaspoon dried oregano

½ teaspoon ground cinnamon

¼ teaspoon ground cloves

1 cup red wine (use something you would happily drink)

2 tablespoons balsamic vinegar

1 (5.5-ounce) can tomato paste

1 teaspoon honey

½ cup water

For Horseradish Mashed Potatoes

2 pounds Yukon Gold potatoes, peeled and quartered

1 tablespoon unsalted butter, room temperature

2 tablespoons prepared or fresh horseradish

1 teaspoon sea salt

ground black pepper, to taste

½ cup–1 cup warm milk or warm vegetable broth

For Serving

steamed spinach or steamed kale (optional)

> **MAKE AHEAD**
>
> *Mushroom Stifado:* 3 days.
>
> *Horseradish Mashed Potatoes:* 3 days.

Make the Mushroom Stifado: In a large pot or dutch oven, heat butter over medium. Add mushrooms, onions, garlic, salt, herbs, and spices. Cook over medium heat, stirring often for 10–15 minutes, gently breaking the onion quarters into individual layers. Increase heat to medium-high, pour in wine and vinegar; boil for 1 minute. Add tomato paste and honey, stirring well to combine, followed by water; mix. Return to a boil, reduce to a simmer, cover, and cook for 45 minutes, stirring every 10–15 minutes.

Make the Mashed Potatoes: Add potatoes to a large pot and cover with 2- to 3-inches of water. Bring to a boil and cook, uncovered, over medium until tender (15–20 minutes). Drain and return to pot and mash. Mix in butter followed by horseradish, salt, and pepper. Slowly add milk or broth until desired consistency. Reheat over low, stirring often.

To Serve: To bowls, add a bed of potatoes, making a gentle well; spoon over stifado. Add a side of steamed spinach or kale (if using). Serve.

MISO MEAL IN A BOWL

Inspired by ramen bowls, this soothing Japanese soup (although, I hesitate to call this "soup" because it's far more robust) is just the thing to annihilate an umami craving. I know it's easy to be turned off by the panoply of ingredients and preparations (which really don't take all that long), but it's important that each are kept separate and assembled immediately before serving. However, most of the components can be made ahead, so you can whip it up in a matter of minutes when a noodle bowl hankering strikes by rehydrating those wispy, cellophane noodles (my kind of pasta, taking 2 minutes max), cubing up some tofu, and reheating the vegetables and broth.

Serves 4

For the Sweet Potatoes and Broccoli

2 pounds (2 large or 4 small) sweet potatoes, peel intact, cut into ½-inch rounds

1 tablespoon refined avocado oil or extra-virgin olive oil

1 tablespoon toasted sesame oil

sea salt, to taste

1 head broccoli, cut into small florets (leave some water clinging)

For the Miso Mushroom Broth

4 cups water

4 portobello mushrooms, stemmed and thinly sliced

1 tablespoon grated fresh ginger

¼ cup white miso

2 tablespoons tamari, plus more for serving

For Serving

½ pound rice vermicelli (brown or white)

1 (7-ounce) package smoked tofu, drained and cubed

sesame seeds

chili flakes

MAKE AHEAD

Sweet Potatoes and Broccoli: 3 days.

Miso Mushroom Broth: 1 week.

Make the Sweet Potatoes and Broccoli: Preheat oven to 400°F. On half of a large-rimmed baking sheet, toss sweet potatoes with oils and salt. Roast in a single layer for 30 minutes, flip, add broccoli to other half of baking sheet, and roast for 10–15 minutes longer.

Make the Miso Mushroom Broth: In a large pot, combine water with mushrooms and ginger. Bring to a boil, reduce to a simmer, partially cover, and cook for 15 minutes. In a small bowl, whisk miso, tamari, and a ladle of warm broth; add to mushroom broth. Keep hot over medium/medium-low heat.

To Serve: Rehydrate noodles with boiling water according to package directions (1–2 minutes maximum); drain. To bowls, add a nest of noodles in center. Around noodles, arrange a fan of sweet potatoes, broccoli, and tofu. Ladle hot broth over bowls (about 1 cup per bowl), being sure to include mushrooms. Garnish with sesame seeds and chili flakes. Serve with tamari for seasoning.

PURPLE VEGETABLE RICE BOWL

This recipe came about after realizing that my refrigerator was beginning to look a bit . . . purple. Gradients of amethyst vegetables really pop when composed, so I couldn't help but combine them all in one recipe. The sweetness of the beets plays gorgeously off the bitter radicchio, mustardy radishes, and aromatic roasted hazelnuts. This is what I imagine a "classic" bowl to be when using **The Whole Bowls Formula**—it has all of those stock formulaic elements, using what you have on hand. Make it a green bowl, orange bowl, red bowl, or any other color you desire with your favorite assortment of similarly hued produce.

Serves 1

For the Bowls

1 beet, kept whole

½ cup water

¼ cup uncooked short grain brown rice

½ cup cooked chickpeas

½ cup finely shredded red cabbage

4 radishes, quartered

¼ head radicchio, cored and cut into wedges

¼ cup roasted hazelnuts, roughly chopped (see page **206**)

2 sprigs fresh cilantro

For the Dressing

2 tablespoons coconut milk

2 teaspoons roasted hazelnut oil or extra-virgin olive oil

2 teaspoons lemon juice

¼ teaspoon sea salt

ground black pepper, to taste

For Serving

balsamic vinegar or Balsamic Glaze (see page **197**)

Make the Roasted Beet and Brown Rice: Preheat oven to 400°F. For roasted beet, crunch beet up in foil and roast for 1–2 hours, or until tender when pierced with a knife. When cool enough to handle, unwrap beet, remove top and bottom, and slice into wedges.

For the brown rice, in a small saucepan, bring water and rice to a boil, reduce to a simmer, cover, and cook for 45 minutes. Steam, covered for 5 minutes; fluff with fork before serving.

Make the Dressing: In a small bowl, whisk all dressing ingredients.

To Serve: To a bowl, add sections of cooked brown rice, roasted beet, chickpeas, cabbage, radishes, and radicchio; pour over dressing. Top with hazelnuts and cilantro. Serve with balsamic vinegar or glaze.

> **MAKE AHEAD**
>
> *Assembled Bowl:* 2 days.
>
> *Brown Rice:* 3 days.
>
> *Roasted Beet:* 1 week.
>
> *Dressing:* 1 week.

> **NOTES**
>
> If you don't like the warm/cold concept of this bowl, the chickpeas, cabbage, radishes, and radicchio can be lightly steamed or sautéed to warm through.

BLACK BEANS WITH BUTTERNUT SQUASH, BLACK RICE, AND CHIMICHURRI

Glossy black rice that's so inky, it almost looks purple, along with its matte counterpart in the form of stewed black beans, the tangerine flesh of butternut squash, and a verdant chimichurri, all come together as edible art.

Serves 4, with extra Chimichurri

For the Butternut Squash

1 (2-pound) butternut squash, peeled, seeded, and cut into ½-inch cubes

1 tablespoon extra-virgin olive oil

½ teaspoon sea salt

ground black pepper, to taste

For the Black Beans

4 cups cooked black beans

1 cup vegetable broth or water

2 teaspoons red wine vinegar

2 teaspoons ground cumin

½ teaspoon smoked paprika

½ teaspoon sea salt

For the Chimichurri

1 clove garlic

1 cup packed fresh cilantro, tender stems included

1 cup packed fresh parsley

5 scallions, roughly chopped

2 tablespoons lemon juice

2 tablespoons red wine vinegar

1 teaspoon sea salt

¼ teaspoon chili flakes, more or less to taste

⅓ cup extra-virgin olive oil

For Serving

2 cups hot, cooked black rice (see page **209**)

MAKE AHEAD

Black Rice: 2 days.

Chimichurri: 3 days. Store with a thin layer of olive oil on top to preserve vibrant green color.

Black Beans: 5 days.

Butternut Squash: 5 days.

Make the Butternut Squash: Preheat oven to 400°F. On a large-rimmed baking sheet, toss squash with oil, salt, and pepper. Roast for 25 to 30 minutes, until tender and beginning to brown.

Make the Black Beans: In a large pot, combine all bean ingredients. Bring to a boil, reduce to a simmer, and cook, uncovered, for 10 minutes, stirring a couple of times.

Make the Chimichurri: Pulse garlic in a food processor until minced. Add cilantro, parsley, and scallions; pulse again until chopped. Add lemon juice, vinegar, salt, and chili; blend. With machine running, slowly drizzle in oil, scrape sides, and blend again until smooth.

To Serve: To bowls, add squash, beans, and rice; spoon over chimichurri. Serve.

MACROBIOTIC BOWLS WITH KALE FRIED RICE, TOFU, AND MISO GRAVY

A few years ago, I learned about the macrobiotic diet, emphasizing grains, cooked starchy vegetables, seaweeds, and fermented soy condiments like miso and tamari. It's not a style of eating that I personally adhere to, but it can produce some incredible flavors in the kitchen—an ethos I can fully adopt. This rich, umami-packed bowl proves that "health food" and great taste are not mutually exclusive.

Serves 4

For the Squash and Tofu

1 (2-pound) kabocha squash, seeded, peeled, and cut into ½-inch pieces

1 (12-ounce) package extra-firm tofu, drained, pressed, and cut into 1-inch cubes (see page **206**)

1 tablespoon refined avocado oil or extra-virgin olive oil

2 teaspoons tamari

For the Kale Fried Rice

1 tablespoon coconut oil or extra-virgin olive oil

1 onion, diced

2 cups cooked, cold brown rice (day-old best)

4 cups (about half a bunch) destemmed, finely chopped kale

For the Miso Gravy

1⅓ cups water, divided

2 tablespoons arrowroot flour

2 tablespoons white miso

2 tablespoons tamari

1 tablespoon coconut oil

1 tablespoon lemon juice or unseasoned rice vinegar

2 teaspoons minced fresh ginger

2 teaspoons toasted sesame oil

1 clove garlic, minced

1 teaspoon maple syrup

For Serving

sesame seeds (optional)

pea sprouts (optional)

MAKE AHEAD

Kale Fried Rice: 1 day.

Squash and Tofu: 4 days.

Miso Gravy: 1 week.

Make the Squash and Tofu: Preheat oven to 400°F. Line a large-rimmed baking sheet with parchment paper. Add squash and tofu to prepared baking sheet, and toss with oil and tamari. Roast for 30 minutes, until squash is tender and tofu is puffed.

Make the Kale Fried Rice: In a wok or large high-sided skillet, heat oil over medium-high. Add onion, reduce heat to medium, and sauté until light brown (8–10 minutes). Return heat to medium-high, and add rice and kale, stirring constantly; stir-fry until rice is hot and kale is wilted (3–5 minutes).

(Continued on page 134)

Make the Miso Gravy: In a medium saucepan, whisk ⅓ cup water and arrowroot. Add remaining gravy ingredients and remaining 1 cup water; whisk until combined. Heat over medium-high, whisking constantly until boiling. Reduce to medium, continuing to whisk while it boils for 1 minute.

To Serve: To bowls, add fried rice; top with squash, tofu, and a ladle of gravy. Garnish with sesame seeds and sprouts (if using). Serve.

NOTES

Replace kabocha cubes with butternut squash, carrot, turnip, or sweet potato.

PEANUT TOFU CURRY

If the addition of peanut butter gives you, to quote my vampire-slaying hero, "the wig," don't worry—it simply acts as a natural thickener and enriching element (just be sure to use a natural brand without added sugar to avoid making this taste like dessert). For those with peanut allergies, try sunflower seed, almond, cashew, or soynut butter.

Serves 4

For the Peanut Tofu Curry

1 tablespoon coconut oil

1 onion, thinly sliced

1 tablespoon mild curry powder

½ teaspoon garam masala

2 teaspoons sea salt

1 (14-ounce) can coconut milk (full-fat or light will both work)

2 tablespoons tomato paste

2 tablespoons unsalted natural peanut butter

1 (12-ounce) package extra-firm tofu, drained, patted dry, and cut into ½-inch cubes

1 small or ½ large head cauliflower, cut into bite-sized florets

For Serving

2 cups hot, cooked brown or basmati rice (see page **209**)

chopped peanuts

Make the Peanut Tofu Curry: In a large pot, warm oil over medium heat. Add onion, spices, and salt, and sauté for 8 minutes; remove from heat. Whisk in coconut milk, tomato paste, and peanut butter, return to heat along with tofu and cauliflower; bring to a boil, reduce to a simmer, cover, and cook for 20–25 minutes, stirring a few times throughout.

To Serve: To bowls, add a mound of rice; ladle curry over and sprinkle with peanuts. Serve.

> **MAKE AHEAD**
>
> *Peanut Tofu Curry:* 4 days.

EMERALD BOWLS WITH MOZZARELLA AND PEA HUMMUS

Don't be put off by the gallimaufry of green ingredients in this bowl. For me, green produce symbolizes healthy eating in a way that no other hue of vegetable can. The pleasantly sweet, psychedelic-green pea hummus anchors milky buffalo mozzarella and mild quinoa, standing in as a white canvas for this sea of green.

Serves 4, with leftover Pea Hummus

For the Vegetables and Quinoa

2 medium zucchini, sliced into ½-inch rounds

1 tablespoon extra-virgin olive oil

½ teaspoon sea salt

1 bunch (8 cups) kale, destemmed, torn into bite-sized pieces

2 cups water

1 cup uncooked quinoa

For the Pea Hummus (makes 1½ cups)

1 clove garlic

2 cups frozen, defrosted green peas

¼ cup raw hulled sunflower seeds or raw pumpkin seeds

2 tablespoons lemon juice

1 teaspoon sea salt

¼ cup extra-virgin olive oil

For Serving

4–6 ounces fresh buffalo mozzarella, sliced into ½-inch rounds, room temperature

MAKE AHEAD

Pea Hummus: 2 days.

Vegetables: 3 days.

Quinoa: 5 days.

Make the Vegetables and Quinoa: Preheat oven to 400°F. On a large-rimmed baking sheet, toss zucchini with oil and salt. Roast for 40 minutes, until soft and beginning to brown; remove from oven and toss with kale. Roast for an additional 5 minutes until kale is wilted and bright green.

In a medium saucepan, add water and quinoa. Bring to a boil, reduce to a simmer, cover, and cook for 15 minutes; remove from heat, steam for 5 minutes, and fluff with a fork.

Make the Pea Hummus: In a food processor, pulse garlic until minced. Add peas, seeds, lemon juice, and salt. Blend until smooth, scraping down sides once. With the machine running, slowly drizzle olive oil through the chute until creamy and light green.

To Serve: To bowls, add compartments of quinoa, vegetables, and a fan of mozzarella; top with a generous dollop of pea hummus. Serve.

CARROT RISOTTO WITH RICE OF THE PRAIRIES

A food trend I can whole-heartedly get behind is the deployment of ancient grains in cooking, not only for their health benefits, but also their complex flavor and texture. Here, I've used Rice of the Prairies (whole oat groats) in place of traditional arborio; they're a step less refined than steel cut, and look similar to farro, spelt (both containing gluten, therefore, not safe for those with celiac disease), and brown rice.

Serves 4

For the Carrot Risotto
2 tablespoons extra-virgin olive oil
1 onion, diced
1 clove garlic, minced
1½ teaspoons sea salt
Ground black pepper, to taste
1 teaspoon dried thyme

1 ⅓ cups whole oat groats (Rice of the Prairies)
5 cups carrot juice
1 tablespoon white wine vinegar

For Serving
4 ounces fresh goat cheese, crumbled

½ cup roasted hazelnuts, roughly chopped (see page **206**)
chopped fresh parsley
roasted hazelnut oil or extra-virgin olive oil

NOTES

This is the time to use your best oil for garnishing—employ your fruitiest extra-virgin or richest hazelnut, even a plush truffle oil really makes this dish pop.

Make the Carrot Risotto: In a large high-sided skillet, heat oil over medium. Add onion, garlic, salt, pepper, and thyme; reduce heat to medium-low and sauté for 10 minutes. Add oats, increase heat to medium, and toast grains for 2 minutes. Add half of carrot juice and cook, stirring often, for 20 minutes. Add remaining carrot juice and continue to cook, stirring often, for 35–45 minutes longer, until majority of liquid is absorbed. Stir in vinegar.

To Serve: To bowls, add a bed of risotto; top with cheese, hazelnuts, parsley, and a generous strand of oil. Serve.

TUSCAN BEAN STEW

Tuscans are lovingly referred to as *mangiafagioli*, or bean-eaters, as much of the region's cuisine is based around these humble delights (I believe I'd fit in quite well!). Not only are dried beans available in winter markets, but also fresh from summer markets, making them a year-round staple. This dish is for when only a big bowl of beans will do.

Serves 6

For the Tuscan Bean Stew

2 tablespoons extra-virgin olive oil, plus more for serving

1 onion, chopped

2 cloves garlic, minced

2 carrots, chopped

2 teaspoons dried thyme

1 teaspoon sea salt

ground black pepper, to taste

1 (28-ounce) can whole tomatoes

4 cups cooked Romano beans (cranberry beans) or cooked large bean of choice

1 tablespoon white wine vinegar

1 bunch curly or lacinato kale, destemmed and chopped

MAKE AHEAD

Tuscan Bean Stew: 5 days.

Make the Tuscan Bean Stew: In a large pot, warm oil over medium heat. Add onion, garlic, carrots, thyme, salt, and pepper; sauté for 10 minutes. Add tomatoes, breaking up into small pieces with a wooden spoon, followed by beans and vinegar. Bring to a boil, reduce to a simmer, cover, and cook for 20 minutes. Slightly increase heat, add kale, stirring to incorporate (it takes a moment or so), cooking until kale has completely wilted.

To Serve: Divide amongst bowls and garnish with additional olive oil. Serve.

ROASTED BROCCOLI ORZO WITH BASIL DRESSING

Orzo, the Italian word for barley (likely better known to you as a shape of pasta), is now widely available in gluten-free varieties made with grains like quinoa, corn, and rice. I enjoy the petite pasta as much for warm use as I do chilled and served as a salad, and this recipe is no exception. The ingredients here are simple, fresh, and light, being thrown together in less than 30 minutes. Double or triple the recipe to suit your needs, and change the vegetable component with the seasons, adjusting roasting times accordingly.

Serves 2

For the Roasted Broccoli Orzo

1 cup uncooked gluten-free orzo or whole grain orzo of choice

1 head broccoli, cut into small florets, tender stems included (leave some water clinging)

⅓ cup parmesan, shaved or coarsely grated

For the Basil Dressing

2 tablespoons finely chopped fresh basil

2 tablespoons lemon juice

2 tablespoons extra-virgin olive oil

1 clove garlic, minced

½ teaspoon sea salt

ground black pepper, to taste

Make the Roasted Broccoli Orzo: Bring a large pot of water to a boil; salt well. Preheat oven to 400°F. Cook pasta according to package directions, drain, and add back to pot. Add broccoli to a large-rimmed baking sheet and roast for 15 minutes. Add broccoli to cooked pasta.

Make the Basil Dressing: In a small bowl, combine all ingredients. Add dressing to pasta and broccoli, stirring over medium-low until heated through and garlic is fragrant.

To Serve: Remove for heat and stir in parmesan. Serve.

SUSHI BOWLS WITH BLACK RICE, TERIYAKI TOFU, AND WASABI MAYO DRESSING

There's a particular sushi house about an hour from my home that I've been visiting, going on ten years now. I've eaten sushi nationally and internationally, and I've yet to find a restaurant that holds a candle to this particular sushi house. Alas, I live a touch too far to make going there a regular habit, so I've created a meal-sized bowl to conquer my craving. Tofu is drenched in a simple teriyaki sauce, adding a burnished, natural shellac and syrupiness, complimented by a backdrop of shadowy rice, sturdy bok choy, and silky avocado.

Serves 4

For the Black Rice

2 cups water

1 cup black rice

2 teaspoons toasted sesame oil

For the Teriyaki Tofu

2 tablespoons tamari

1 tablespoon maple syrup or honey

1 tablespoon vegan, gluten-free Worcestershire sauce

1 (12-ounce) package extra-firm tofu, pressed and cut crosswise into ½-inch slices (see page **208**)

For the Wasabi Mayo Dressing

⅓ cup mayonnaise (see page **198**)

2 tablespoons lime juice

1 tablespoon white miso

2 teaspoons dried wasabi powder or prepared wasabi

For Serving

1 pound steamed greens (whole baby bok choy, spinach, rapini, and broccoli florets all work well)

2 avocados, halved, pitted, and sliced

2 sheets nori, torn

white sesame seeds

MAKE AHEAD

Black Rice: 2 days.

Teriyaki Tofu: 4 days.

Wasabi Mayo Dressing: 1 week.

Make the Black Rice: In a medium saucepan, bring water and rice to a boil, reduce to a simmer, cover, and cook for 45 minutes. Remove from heat and steam, covered, for 5 minutes. Stir in sesame oil.

Make the Teriyaki Tofu: Preheat oven to 400°F. For sauce, in small bowl, combine tamari, honey, and Worcestershire. Line a large-rimmed baking sheet with parchment paper, add tofu in a single layer, and evenly coat with sauce. Bake for 20 minutes.

Make the Wasabi Mayo Dressing: In a small bowl, whisk all dressing ingredients until blended. Refrigerate until ready to serve.

To Serve: To bowls, add a mound of rice at bottom; top with a fan of tofu, a side of steamed greens, half an avocado per bowl, and nestle in a few shards of nori. Drizzle with dressing and sprinkle with sesame seeds. Serve.

CHILI CON VEGGIE WITH CORNBREAD

Chili and cornbread don't make quite the splashy entrance like some of the other bowls in this cookbook, and they're not supposed to. They're the comfy, reliable, stress-free guys that everyone loves. This veggie-rich bowl reheats perfectly for lunches or dinners in the days to come. In fact, I think it even benefits from a snooze in the refrigerator overnight.

Serves 5

For the Chili

2 tablespoons extra-virgin olive oil

2 onions, chopped

1 bell pepper, seeded and chopped into 1-inch cubes

3 cloves garlic, minced

1 tablespoon chili powder

2 teaspoons sea salt

1 teaspoon coriander seed

1 teaspoon smoked paprika

1 teaspoon dried oregano

1 (5.5-ounce) can tomato paste

1 (28-ounce) can whole tomatoes

2 tablespoons lime juice

2 cups cooked mixed beans and/or lentils (white kidney beans (cannellini beans), red kidney beans, black beans, green lentils, etc.)

1 (8-ounce) package tempeh, crumbled

¾ cup water

For the Cornbread

1 cup chickpea flour

1 cup fine cornmeal, plus extra for pan

1 tablespoon evaporated cane sugar or coconut sugar

2 teaspoons baking powder

1 teaspoon baking soda

1 teaspoon sea salt

1½ cups water

2 tablespoons extra-virgin olive oil, plus extra for pan

1 tablespoon apple cider vinegar

For Serving

avocado slices

diced scallions

fresh cilantro

MAKE AHEAD

Cornbread: 1 day.

Chili: 1 week; 2 months, frozen.

Make the Chili: In a large pot or dutch oven, warm oil over medium heat. Add onions, peppers, garlic, chili powder, salt, coriander, paprika, and oregano; sauté for 8–10 minutes. Stir in tomato paste, followed by tomatoes, breaking apart with a wooden spoon. Mix in lime juice, beans, tempeh, and water. Bring to boil, reduce to a simmer, cover, and cook for 25 to 30 minutes, stirring once or twice.

Make the Cornbread: Preheat oven to 375°F. Grease an 8- or 9-inch cast-iron skillet or 8x8-inch square baking pan with oil, coat bottom and sides with cornmeal, shake out extra. In a large bowl, mix chickpea flour, cornmeal, sugar, baking powder and soda, and salt. Whisk in water, oil, and vinegar. Pour into prepared pan and bake for 15–20 minutes, until a toothpick inserted in the center comes out clean.

To Serve: Ladle chili into bowls; garnish with avocado, scallions, and cilantro. Slice wedges or squares of cornbread for serving on the side (or on top). Serve.

ROASTED FENNEL AND PEA TRI-GRAIN PENNE WITH HAZELNUTS

On a weekend trip to New Orleans, Louisiana, I dined at the famed Restaurant August, where fennel was presented to me as the star of my entrée. With this meal, I learned that fennel's paleness—both in hue and taste—pairs best with other muted ingredients. And, like many vegetables, fennel's excellence is teased out by certain cutting and cooking techniques: paper-thin slices for raw use, thin for quicker roasting (as I've done here), and quartered for slower roasting and braising.

Serves 4

1 bulb fennel, cored, quartered and thinly sliced (including green fronds)

3 cloves garlic, slivered

2 tablespoons extra-virgin olive oil

¾ pound gluten-free tri-grain penne (look for a brown rice, amaranth, and corn blend) or whole grain penne of choice

1 cup reserved pasta cooking water

½ cup white wine

1 cup fresh or frozen, defrosted green peas

½ cup roasted hazelnuts, chopped (see page **206**)

½ teaspoon sea salt, plus more for pasta water

ground black pepper, to taste

grated parmesan, for serving

Preheat oven to 350°F.

Make the Roasted Fennel: On a large-rimmed baking sheet, combine fennel, garlic, and oil. Roast for 45 minutes.

Make the Pasta: Bring a large pot of water to a boil; salt well. Cook pasta according to package directions, reserve 1 cup cooking water, and drain. Add wine to pasta cooking pot and bring to a boil. To wine, add roasted fennel and garlic, peas, hazelnuts, salt, pepper, and cooked pasta. Reduce to medium and cook, stirring constantly, adding pasta water until desired consistency and mixture is heated through.

To Serve: Add pasta to bowls and serve with parmesan at the table.

BAKED POLENTA WITH CARAMELIZED ONIONS, MUSHROOMS, AND MARINARA

This bowl was created with my sister, Kirsten, in mind, combining all of her favorites in one snug entrée. In the spirit of her disdain for cooking, I've included a couple of store-bought options for the polenta and marinara, cutting the work in half without compromising the taste.

Serves 4–5

For the Polenta or use 1 log premade polenta

5 cups water

1½ cups fine polenta (cornmeal)

1 teaspoon sea salt

olive oil, for brushing

For the Caramelized Onions and Mushrooms

2 tablespoons extra-virgin olive oil

1½ pounds (about 9 cups, sliced) mixed mushrooms (cremini, portobella, and button all work well), quartered if small, or sliced into ½-inch pieces if large

1½ pounds (about 5 cups or 4 large) onions, halved and sliced into ¼-inch half moons

2 teaspoons maple syrup

2 teaspoons chopped fresh or dried rosemary

1 teaspoon sea salt

For the Marinara or use 1 (24-ounce) jar premade marinara sauce

1 tablespoon extra-virgin olive oil

1 onion, diced

1 carrot, diced

1 clove garlic, minced

½ teaspoon sea salt

1 (28-ounce) can whole tomatoes

1 fresh basil leaf

Make the Polenta: Add a splash of water to an 8x8-inch square baking pan, rolling to coat bottom. To a large pot, add water, polenta, and salt, whisking to combine. Whisking constantly, bring to a boil, reduce to low, cover, and cook for 5 minutes. Remove from heat and wait for polenta to stop boiling before lifting lid. Uncover, whisk well, pour into prepared pan, smooth top, cover, and refrigerate for 1–2 hours or until solidified. (Use this time to prepare the remaining components.)

To bake polenta before serving, preheat oven to 425°F. Line a large-rimmed baking sheet with parchment paper. Slice polenta into 4 large squares, followed by an "X" in each of the 4 squares, for 16 triangles. Line polenta triangles on prepared baking sheet and brush with olive oil. If using store-bought polenta, slice into 1-inch rounds, line on prepared baking sheet, and brush with oil. Bake for 20 minutes.

MAKE AHEAD

Polenta: 1 week.

Caramelized Onions and Mushrooms: 1 week.

Marinara: 1 week; 2 months, frozen.

Make the Caramelized Onions and Mushrooms: In a large high-sided skillet or large pot, warm oil over medium heat. Add mushrooms, onions, maple syrup, rosemary, and salt; sauté over medium-low heat for 30–40 minutes, or until vegetables are very soft and light brown.

Make the Marinara: In a medium saucepan, warm oil over medium heat. Add onion, carrot, garlic, and salt; sauté for 8–10 minutes, until soft. Add tomatoes and basil, breaking up tomatoes with a wooden spoon. Bring to a boil, reduce to a simmer, cover, and cook for 10–15 minutes. If not using immediately, reheat before serving. If using jarred sauce, add to a medium saucepan and cook over medium until heated through.

To Serve: To bowls, add a couple of ladles of sauce; fan polenta wedges in center and drape over onions and mushrooms. Serve.

SPICE ROUTE BOWLS WITH SWEET POTATO COINS, MILLET COUSCOUS, AND GOLDEN CURRY PECAN SAUCE

The best way to add kick to a plant-based meal is by a heavy-handed application of Moroccan spices. The vibrant colors and heady aroma they give off work wonders to make a dish seem extraordinarily glamorous. Spices are also packed with anti-inflammatory and digestive benefits, along with being a rich source of antioxidants. I've served this with couscous, traditionally made of wheat, but replaced here with gluten-free millet. A hearty, healthy bowl that looks and tastes desert-sun-kissed.

Serves 4

For the Sweet Potato Coins

2 pounds (2 large or 4 small) sweet potatoes, peel intact, cut into ½-inch rounds

1 tablespoon coconut oil or extra-virgin olive oil

½ teaspoon sea salt

For the Millet Couscous

1 tablespoon extra-virgin olive oil

1 cup uncooked millet

2 cups water

1 teaspoon sea salt

2 cups cooked chickpeas

1 cup chopped fresh parsley or cilantro

¼ cup dried currants or raisins

4 scallions, diced

For the Golden Curry Pecan Sauce

¾ cup very hot, recently boiled water

1 clove garlic, minced

½ cup unsalted pecan halves

1 tablespoon curry powder (mild or hot)

1 tablespoon lemon juice

2 teaspoons maple syrup

1 teaspoon sea salt

MAKE AHEAD

Sweet Potato Coins: 3 days.

Millet Couscous: 3 days.

Golden Curry Pecan Sauce: 3 days.

Make the Sweet Potato Coins: Preheat oven to 400°F. On a large-rimmed baking sheet, coat sweet potatoes with oil and salt, and spread in a single layer. Roast for 20 minutes, flip, and roast for an additional 20 minutes, or until tender.

Make the Millet Couscous: In a medium saucepan, warm oil over medium-high heat; add millet and toast, stirring constantly, for 1–2 minutes. Add water and salt; bring to a boil, reduce to a simmer, cover, and cook for 25 minutes (do not stir during cooking time or it will turn creamy). Remove from heat and steam, covered, for 5 minutes. Fluff with a fork and gently incorporate chickpeas, cilantro, currants or raisins, and scallions.

Make the Golden Curry Pecan Sauce: Add all sauce ingredients to a blender and blend until creamy.

To Serve: To bowls, add a generous bed of couscous; top with a fan of sweet potatoes and drizzle with sauce. Serve.

PASTA E CECI (CHICKPEA AND PASTA SOUP)

Pasta e ceci, a traditional Roman dish, is the vegetarian's answer to chicken noodle soup. The dish lies somewhere between a stew and soup, with the diminutive pasta soaking up a rich chickpea and vegetable-infused broth until fat with flavor.

Serves 6

For the Pasta e Ceci

2 tablespoons extra-virgin olive oil

2 carrots, chopped

1 onion, chopped

1 teaspoon dried thyme

1 teaspoon sea salt

ground black pepper, to taste

6 cups vegetable stock

2 cups cooked chickpeas

1 cup uncooked gluten-free orzo or small whole grain pasta of choice, such as ditalini

1 tablespoon lemon juice

MAKE AHEAD

Pasta e Ceci: 5 days.

Make the Pasta e Ceci: In a large pot, heat oil over medium. Add carrots, onion, thyme, salt, and pepper; sauté for 10 minutes. Add stock and chickpeas; bring to a boil, reduce to a simmer, cover, and cook for 5 minutes. Return to a boil, stir in orzo and lemon juice, reduce to a simmer, cover, and cook for 8–10 minutes, until pasta is cooked.

To Serve: Ladle into bowls. Serve.

LOADED BAKED POTATOES WITH BAKED BEANS AND THE WORKS

Potatoes are nature's bowls, so why not employ them to do what they do best? As I like my baked potatoes with "the works," you'll notice this recipe is unapologetically messy, not at all dainty. It's filling, hearty, and can transition to the realm of entertaining by setting up an interactive topping bar (which also means less work for you).

Serves 6

For the Baked Potatoes

6 small baking (russet) potatoes

2 teaspoons extra-virgin olive oil or coconut oil

sea salt

For the Baked Beans

2 tablespoons extra-virgin olive oil

2 onions, finely diced

1 (28-ounce) can crushed tomatoes

1 (5.5-ounce) can tomato paste

⅓ cup distilled white vinegar

1 tablespoon maple syrup

1 tablespoon molasses

2 teaspoons sea salt

ground black pepper, to taste

¼ teaspoon ground nutmeg

4 cups cooked white kidney beans (cannellini beans)

The Works

1 cup sour cream

1 cup grated or shaved sharp cheddar cheese

1 cup sliced scallions

Smoked paprika

MAKE AHEAD

Baked Potatoes: 2 days.

Baked Beans: 1 week (with or without baking); 2 months, frozen (unbaked).

Arrange oven racks in top and bottom third of oven to accommodate two trays. Preheat oven to 400°F.

Make the Baked Potatoes: On a large-rimmed baking sheet, coat potatoes with oil, sprinkle with salt, and prick each potato a few times with a knife. Set aside until the beans are ready to go in the oven along with the potatoes.

Make the Baked Beans: In a large pot or dutch oven, heat oil over medium. Add onion and sauté until beginning to brown (about 15 minutes); remove from heat. Add remaining ingredients except beans, whisking to combine; mix in beans. Keep in the pot or dutch oven and cover with a lid, or transfer mixture to a large ovenproof dish and cover tightly with foil.

Add beans to bottom rack of oven and potatoes to top rack of oven. Cook for 1–1½ hours, until potatoes are tender when pierced with a knife and beans are bubbling.

To Serve: Place potatoes in the center of bowls. Make a cross with a knife and open the potatoes up to create potato "bowls." Drape baked beans over baked potatoes (don't forget to scrape the sides for the caramelized sauce), followed by desired toppings. Serve.

ROASTED VEGETABLE BOWLS WITH FRIED EGGS AND GOAT CHEESE

I make this bowl on a weekly basis. It's comforting, quick, and I can use seasonal vegetables (or remnants of past prime ones) to suit my tastes. Switch up the spices, grains, and cheeses to suit your mood. The starchy vegetables that take longer to cook are cut smaller, while the ones that cook more quickly are kept chunkier—be sure to keep this in mind when mixing and matching the produce so you don't get an overcooked/undercooked bowl.

Serves 4

For the Roasted Vegetables

1 (2-pound) butternut squash, peeled, seeded, cut into ½-inch cubes

1 head broccoli, cut into florets

1 cup cherry or grape tomatoes

2 tablespoons extra-virgin olive oil

1 teaspoon sea salt

ground black pepper, to taste

1 teaspoon dried thyme

For Serving

extra-virgin olive oil

4 large eggs

2 cups hot, cooked grain of choice (see page **209**)

4 ounces fresh goat cheese, crumbled

balsamic vinegar or Balsamic Glaze (see page **198**)

MAKE AHEAD

Roasted Vegetables: 3 days.

Make the Roasted Vegetables: Preheat oven to 400°F. On large-rimmed baking sheet, toss together all roasted vegetable ingredients. Roast for 40–45 minutes.

Fry the Eggs: Immediately before serving, to a large non-stick skillet, add a splash of olive oil. Crack in eggs. Fry until desired cook.

To Serve: To bowls, add a bed of grains; top with roasted vegetables, egg, and cheese. Drizzle with balsamic vinegar. Serve.

ORECCHIETTE WITH SOUR BEETS, RICOTTA, AND POPPY SEEDS

Orecchiette's cupped shape is ideal for catching sturdier sauces like this earthy (addictive) beet-based one. Its flavors are slightly Eastern European (think borscht), with a power punch of vinegar to keep it out of the overly sweet category. Ricotta and poppy seeds can be switched with what's on-hand—try thick yogurt or goat cheese for the creamy component, and chopped toasted almonds or walnuts for the crunch.

.... *Serves 4–6* ....

2 tablespoons extra-virgin olive oil

1 pound (about 4 small) beets, grated

1 onion, diced

2 cloves garlic, minced

¾ teaspoon sea salt

ground black pepper, to taste

1 tablespoon balsamic vinegar

¾ pound gluten-free orecchiette or fusilli, or whole grain orecchiette or fusilli choice

½ cup reserved pasta cooking water

1 cup whole milk ricotta

1 tablespoon poppy seeds

Bring a large pot of water to a boil; salt well.

Make the Beets: In a high-sided skillet, heat oil over medium. Add beets, onion, garlic, salt, and pepper. Sauté 10–15 minutes, until softened. Stir in vinegar.

Make the Pasta: Cook pasta according to package directions, reserve ½ cup cooking liquid, and drain. Add pasta back to pot along with cooked beet mixture. Briefly stir over medium until heated through, adding reserved pasta cooking water to loosen, as required.

To Serve: Add pasta to bowls, top with a dollop of ricotta, and sprinkle with poppy seeds. Serve.

DOUBLE GRAIN WILD MUSHROOM RISOTTO

The redolence, meaty chew, and earth tones of wild mushrooms can really stand up to brown rice and oat groats—two often overlooked whole grains, themselves adding a soft, putty hue for a bit more drama. A quick heads-up before you tie on your apron: be sure not to discard the murky mushroom soaking liquid; it's packed with a deep, umami essence and used as part of the cooking liquid amount.

Serves 4

For the Double Grain Wild Mushroom Risotto

½ ounce dried porcini or dried mixed wild mushrooms, chopped (chopping may be easier after rehydrating, depending on mushroom variety)

1 cup recently boiled water

2 tablespoons extra-virgin olive oil

¾ pound cremini mushrooms, sliced

1 onion, diced

1 clove garlic, minced

1 cup oat groats (Rice of the Prairies)

½ cup short grain brown rice

3 cups vegetable stock

2 tablespoons white wine vinegar

½ teaspoon sea salt

ground black pepper, to taste

For Serving

sliced fresh basil

MAKE AHEAD

Double Grain Wild Mushroom Risotto: 3 days.

NOTES

If making ahead, adding a splash of additional vegetable stock or water when reheating will help return this to its just-made consistency. If using water, you'll likely have to add a touch of extra salt.

Make the Double Grain Wild Mushroom Risotto: In a medium bowl, rehydrate dried mushrooms with water for 20 minutes. Save liquid, remove mushrooms.

In a large pot or large high-sided skillet, heat oil over medium heat. Add cremini and rehydrated porcini mushrooms, onion, and garlic; sauté for 10 minutes. Increase heat to high, add oats and rice, stirring to coat, followed by reserved mushroom liquid and 1 cup stock. Bring to a boil, reduce to a simmer, cover, and cook for 20 minutes. Remove lid, add remaining stock, salt, and pepper; bring back to a boil, reduce to medium, and cook uncovered for 30 minutes, stirring often.

To Serve: Spoon into bowls and top with a light scattering of basil. Serve.

MAC AND CHEESE WITH SMOKED TOFU AND BAKED TOMATOES

I was inspired to create this vegan, nut-free macaroni and "cheese" after tasting a version (stolen off my sister's plate) at the celebrated plant-based restaurant Graze in Vancouver, British Columbia, Canada. While their version contained coconut milk, I've used soy milk for a more neutral base; the cheesiness comes from nutritional yeast; and a little smoked tofu, which adds a bacon-like quality to the dish, is the pièce de résistance. (Graze made their divine smoked tofu in-house, but at home, I buy it.) To add a bright contrast to the rich base, sweet tomatoes with a cornmeal crunch (a faux "gratin," if you will) bring this cozy meal together. Put on a sweater, find a big bowl, and dive in.

Serves 6

For the Cheese Sauce
½ cup water
¼ cup arrowroot flour
2 cups unsweetened plain soy milk
⅓ cup nutritional yeast
2 tablespoons coconut oil
1 tablespoon Dijon mustard
1 clove garlic, minced or ½ teaspoon garlic powder
2 teaspoons sea salt
ground black pepper, to taste

½ teaspoon turmeric
⅛ teaspoon ground nutmeg

For the Baked Tomatoes
3 field tomatoes, halved
½ cup cornmeal
1 tablespoon extra-virgin olive oil
½ teaspoon sea salt
½ teaspoon dried thyme
¼ teaspoon garlic powder

For the Pasta and Tofu
3 cups (10 ounces) uncooked gluten-free brown rice macaroni noodles
1 (7-ounce) package smoked tofu, drained and cut into ½-inch cubes (see *Notes*)

MAKE AHEAD

Cheese Sauce: 5 days; 2 months, frozen.

Bring a large pot of water to a boil; salt well. Preheat oven to 400°F.

Make the Cheese Sauce: In a medium saucepan, whisk water and arrowroot; whisk in remaining sauce ingredients. Whisking constantly, bring to a boil over medium heat. Once bubbling and thick, continue to whisk over medium for 1–2 minutes. Remove from heat.

(Continued on page 166)

Make the Baked Tomatoes: Line tomatoes cut-side up on a greased or parchment-lined baking sheet. In a small bowl, combine cornmeal, oil, salt, thyme, and garlic powder. Top each tomato half with some of cornmeal mixture. Bake in preheated oven for 25–30 minutes, until bubbling and crispy.

Make the Pasta: Cook pasta according to package directions (7–8 minutes for most gluten-free macaroni); drain (do not rinse). Add back to pot along with prepared sauce and smoked tofu. Cook over medium heat, stirring constantly, until heated through.

To Serve: To bowls, add prepared pasta; top with a tomato half. Serve.

> **NOTES**
>
> Smoked tofu is essential for both flavor and texture; most supermarkets stock it next to regular fresh tofu. If you can't find it, coat an equal amount of extra-firm tofu in oil, smoked paprika, and salt, then bake or stir-fry until crispy.
>
> By itself, the sauce can be draped over steamed cauliflower and broccoli, or used as a dairy-free (and lightened up) hollandaise for asparagus or eggs.

THAI GREEN COCONUT CURRY WITH TOFU AND BOK CHOY

Green vegetable curry has been the only thing I've ordered at Thai restaurants for years. At home, I purchase premade vegan and gluten-free green curry paste to recreate the dish in my own kitchen. If you have access to some of the more exotic ingredients the fiery paste ordinarily contains, feel free to make you own.

Serves 4

For the Green Coconut Curry

1 tablespoon coconut oil

3–4 tablespoons green curry paste (vegan, gluten-free)

1 (14-ounce) can full-fat coconut milk

1 tablespoon lime juice

1 teaspoon sea salt

1 (12-ounce) package extra-firm tofu, drained (pressed, if you have time) and cut into 1-inch cubes (see page **208**)

1 pound baby bok choy, halved or 1 head broccoli, cut into florets

1 red bell pepper, cut into 1-inch cubes

½ cup whole fresh basil leaves, halved

For Serving

2 cups hot, cooked short grain brown, jasmine, or basmati rice (see page **209**)

unsweetened coconut flakes or unsweetened shredded coconut

MAKE AHEAD

Green Coconut Curry: 4 days.

Make the Green Coconut Curry: In a large pot or wok, heat oil over medium heat. Add curry paste, stirring until fragrance releases (about 30 seconds). Stir in coconut milk, lime juice, and salt; bring to a boil. Mix in tofu, bok choy or broccoli, and pepper. Return to a boil, reduce to medium, cover, and cook, stirring halfway through, for 10–15 minutes, or until vegetables are tender-crisp. Stir in basil immediately before serving.

To Serve: To bowls, add a bed of rice; ladle curry over and sprinkle with coconut. Serve.

SAFFRON, BUTTERNUT, AND BEAN STEW WITH HARISSA YOGURT

Infused with saffron and orange, this Moroccan-inspired stew will impart the incredible aromas of North Africa into your kitchen. The garlic becomes sweet and mellow once stewed so don't be afraid of the amount. Leftovers reheat beautifully for lunch the following day.

.... *Serves 5* ....

For the Saffron, Butternut, and Bean Stew

2 tablespoons extra-virgin olive oil

2 cups butternut squash, cut in ½-inch cubes

2 onions, halved, sliced into thin ribbons

2 teaspoons sea salt

ground black pepper, to taste

2 teaspoons dried thyme

1 teaspoon ground cumin

¼ teaspoon saffron

4 cloves garlic, minced

½ cup orange juice

1 (28-ounce) can whole or diced tomatoes

2 cups cooked white kidney beans or white navy beans (great northern beans)

1¼ cups water or vegetable broth

2 cups kale, cored and cut into ribbons

For the Harissa Yogurt

½ cup whole milk plain yogurt, preferably Greek

1 tablespoon harissa paste (see page **197**)

For Serving

toasted pine nuts or slivered toasted almonds

Make the Saffron, Butternut, and Bean Stew: In a large pot or dutch oven, warm oil over medium heat. Add squash, onions, salt, pepper, thyme, cumin, and saffron. Sauté for 15 minutes, until vegetables are tender. Add garlic; cook for 1 minute longer. Add remaining stew ingredients except kale. Roughly break up tomatoes with a wooden spoon. Bring to a boil, reduce to simmer, cover, and cook for 30 minutes.

Make the Harissa Yogurt: In a small bowl, stir together harissa and yogurt. Refrigerate until ready to serve.

To Serve: Stir kale into stew and cook until wilted. Ladle into bowls, dollop with yogurt, and top with pine nuts or almonds. Serve.

MAKE AHEAD

Harissa Yogurt: 1 week.

Saffron, Butternut, and Bean Stew: 1 week; 2 months, frozen.

MEDITERRANEAN PASTA WITH ARUGULA, PEAS, YELLOW TOMATOES, AND FETA

This main has a fresh, springy, Mediterranean flavor profile: a spectrum of tastes I rely on in my everyday kitchen for a dish that doesn't swerve. Slicked with lustrous olive oil, polka dotted with midnight purple kalamata olives, strewn with wisps of arugula, and backed by the Pantry Prince, dried oregano, the tendrils of pasta practically beg to be twirled into a plump reel on your fork.

Serves 4

For the Pasta

1 pound gluten-free spaghetti or linguini, or whole grain spaghetti or linguini of choice

½ cup reserved pasta cooking water

⅓ cup white wine

¼ cup extra-virgin olive oil

2 cloves garlic, minced

2 teaspoons dried oregano

¾ teaspoon sea salt

ground black pepper, to taste

1 pound yellow or red tomatoes, sliced into wedges

5 ounces (6–8 cups) arugula

1 cup fresh or frozen, defrosted green peas

1 cup pitted kalamata olives, left whole or halved

For Serving

4 ounces feta cheese, crumbled

Make the Pasta: Bring a large pot of water to a boil; salt well. Cook pasta according to package directions (7–8 minutes for most gluten-free varieties). Reserve ½ cup pasta cooking water. Drain and rinse with very hot tap water (skip rinsing if using regular, non-gluten-free pasta). In the same large pot, add wine, oil, garlic, oregano, salt, and pepper; bring to a boil, reduce heat to medium, add back cooked pasta, and toss to combine. Loosen sauce with reserved pasta cooking water. Add in remaining ingredients except feta; briefly cook until heated through.

To Serve: To bowls, add pasta; top with feta. Serve.

Chapter 4: Dessert Whole Bowls

Like many kids, I started out in the kitchen helping my mom with some home baking; my specialties were simple things that required a lot of stirring like muffins, cakes, and cookies. I graduated to following a recipe on my own (but not yet to washing dishes, to her displeasure), rolled up my sleeves, and continued to love the act of measuring, kitchen chemistry, and perfectibility that goes hand-in-hand with baking and desserts.

Though I don't consider myself a fine-tuned or overly adventurous baker, I do love to eat desserts, and much of the point of making sweets is about sharing the sweetness with others.

The recipes you'll find in here aren't complicated, but many do capitalize on the necessity of baking when things in life are less frenetic—meaning, some of my dessert recipes, like many dessert recipes, take time to cook or bake and cool. (They say patience is a virtue, but I'm on the fence.) However, I haven't forgotten about the rushed times, so there are a few gems in here for those occasions too; those occasions being my, and I'm guessing your, every day.

For serving, more diminutive bowls are used (less The Big Bowl of Cookie Dough), but that doesn't mean you can't go back for seconds or thirds. Sweets are one of life's unwavering delights, so go on, try a few, you deserve it, just because.

DESSERT WHOLE BOWLS

MEXICAN CHOCOLATE PUDDING
176

CARROT CAKE WITH CREAM CHEESE DOLLOP AND
CANDIED CARROTS
179

ANYTIME PEACH BUCKWHEAT CRISP
181

BUMBLEBERRY PIE WITH ALL-BUTTER PASTRY
183

THE BIG BOWL OF COOKIE DOUGH
184

SUNNY CITRUS BOWLS WITH ORANGE POMEGRANATE SALSA
AND LEMON CREAM
187

DANISH RISALAMANDE WITH CARDAMOM CHERRIES
189

ROASTED PEARS WITH WHIPPED GOAT CHEESE AND
MAPLE PINE NUT BRITTLE
191

MINT CHOCOLATE STRACCIATELLA GELATO
192

MEXICAN CHOCOLATE PUDDING

The simplicity of chocolate pudding never goes out of style; however, spiced with cinnamon and cayenne, it instantly feels a touch more extraordinary. This is a wickedly tricky way to use up ripe avocados (but I promise you won't taste their vegetal undertones) and can be topped with even more kitchen chicanery in the form of a faux whipped cream made from canned coconut milk. High in healthy fats (and deliciousness), along with an array of other nutrients, this is a bowl you'll want to hug.

.... *Serves 2* ....

For the Mexican Chocolate Pudding

⅔ cup unsweetened plain almond milk

¼ cup maple syrup

¼ cup unsweetened cocoa powder

1 teaspoon vanilla extract

1 teaspoon ground cinnamon

⅛ to ¼ teaspoon cayenne pepper

pinch, sea salt

2 ripe avocados, pitted and flesh scooped out

Topping Ideas

cacao nibs

cinnamon and/or cayenne

chopped hazelnuts

coconut Dreamy Whip (see page **204**)

coconut flakes

fresh fruit

Make the Mexican Chocolate Pudding: In a food processor or blender, add all ingredients in the order listed. Blend until smooth and creamy, scrape down sides, and blend again. Transfer to a bowl, cover, and chill for at least 1 hour, or until very cold.

To Serve: To bowls, add pudding; garnish with any of the suggested toppings. Serve.

MAKE AHEAD

Chocolate Pudding: 2 days.

CARROT CAKE WITH CREAM CHEESE DOLLOP AND CANDIED CARROTS

When I was a kid, carrot cake's whole wheat–looking crumb, shredded carrot confetti, and tangy, rich frosting seemed like the most sophisticated dessert there was and ever would be. I still have my mom's recipe for the "Lunchbox Carrot Cake" I enjoyed as a kid in the nineties, written with a blue ballpoint pen on a tattered, water-smudged, tangerine index card. The ingredients and method of her version are different than mine, but the presentation is nearly identical—carrot cake in my house was only to be baked in a rectangular glass dish and cut into squares, never presented as a circular layer cake. I created this recipe with my dad in mind; he's a lifelong carrot cake devotee.

Serves 8

For the Carrot Cake

1 cup quinoa flour

½ cup dark buckwheat flour

⅓ cup coconut sugar or evaporated cane sugar

2 teaspoons ground cinnamon

1 teaspoon ground dried ginger

1½ teaspoons baking powder

1 teaspoon baking soda

½ teaspoon xanthan gum

½ teaspoon sea salt

1 large egg

1 cup unsweetened applesauce

½ cup unsweetened plain almond milk

⅓ cup extra-virgin olive oil, plus more for greasing

1½ cups (1–2 carrots worth) grated carrot

¼ cup raisins (optional)

For the Cream Cheese Dollop

1 cup (8 ounces) cream cheese, room temperature

3 tablespoons honey or maple syrup

1 teaspoon vanilla extract or vanilla bean paste

zest of 1 orange

½ cup coconut oil, melted and cooled (but still liquid)

¼ cup unsweetened plain almond milk, cold

For the Candied Carrots

2 carrots, sliced into ¼-inch rounds

¼ cup orange juice

1 tablespoon honey

For Serving

½ cup chopped pecans or walnuts

MAKE AHEAD

Carrot Cake: 2 days.

Cream Cheese Dollop: 2 days.

Candied Carrots: 2 days.

Make the Carrot Cake: Preheat oven to 325°F. Grease an 8x8-inch square baking pan with oil; set aside. In a large bowl, combine flours, sugar, cinnamon, ginger, baking powder and soda, xanthan gum, and salt. In a medium bowl, whisk together egg, applesauce, milk, and oil; add to flour mixture, stirring to incorporate. Add carrots and raisins (if using) to batter; mix until combined. Transfer to prepared pan and smooth until flat. Bake for 25–30 minutes, until a toothpick inserted in center comes out with just a few damp crumbs; cool completely in pan. Cover and refrigerate in pan for at least 2 hours.

(Continued on page 180)

Make the Cream Cheese Dollop: In a stand mixer fitted with whisk attachment, or in a large bowl with a hand mixer, beat cream cheese, honey or maple syrup, vanilla, and orange zest until creamy, stopping once to scrape down sides and whisk. With mixer running, slowly drizzle in oil; scrape bottom of bowl and sides; beat again briefly. Add milk, beat until incorporated; scrape down bottom of bowl and sides; beat again on high until fluffy and smooth. Transfer to a bowl, cover, and refrigerate for at least 2 hours.

Make the Candied Carrots: In a large skillet, add carrots in a single layer, followed by orange juice and honey. Bring to a boil, reduce to medium-low, cover, and cook for 5 minutes. Uncover, increase heat to medium, and cook until all liquid is reduced. Once all liquid is gone, continue to cook over medium until glossy and beginning to caramelize (5–10 minutes), flipping carrots once. Transfer to a plate to cool. Cover and refrigerate until ready to serve.

To Serve: Slice cake into squares; add to bowls and generously dollop with frosting. Garnish with a tumble of carrots and nuts. Serve.

ANYTIME PEACH BUCKWHEAT CRISP

Summertime's gorgeous peaches—the kind that, when you bite into them, they dribble down your chin and onto your shirt—are sadly only available a few short months of the year. This recipe works wonderfully with unpeeled, sunsoaked fresh peaches; however, baking with a frozen version is a perfectly viable and delectable option during their off-season when you're craving some sunrays in January.

Serves 4

For the Peach Buckwheat Crisp

1½ pounds (about 4 heaping cups) unsweetened frozen (do not defrost), sliced peaches, or fresh, unpeeled, pitted and sliced peaches

⅓ cup coconut oil or unsalted butter, melted

1 cup large flake rolled oats

⅓ cup coconut sugar or evaporated cane sugar

¼ cup plus 2 tablespoons dark buckwheat flour

1 teaspoon ground cinnamon

¼ teaspoon sea salt

For Serving

vanilla ice cream or lightly sweetened whipped cream

Make the Peach Buckwheat Crisp: Preheat oven to 350°F. Add peaches to an 8x8-inch square baking pan or 8-inch pie plate. In a medium bowl, mix remaining crisp ingredients and evenly distribute over peaches. Bake for 40–50 minutes, until juices bubble and top is crispy.

To Serve: To bowls, add crisp (warm or chilled); top with a scoop of ice cream or dollop of whipped cream. Serve.

> **MAKE AHEAD**
>
> *Peach Buckwheat Crisp:* 3 days.

BUMBLEBERRY PIE WITH ALL-BUTTER PASTRY

I feel just so domestically competent when I make dough from scratch. I hear it's easy (which this recipe is—no chilling!), so it's silly I'd avoided making it for most of my life. This particular crust is a sturdier, whole wheat–esque variation, capitalizing on the inherent nuttiness of the grains. And just a quick note: a bumbleberry is not a real berry, so don't go asking for it at the supermarket—not that I've ever tried . . .

Serves 4, with extra All-Butter Pastry

For the All-Butter Pastry

½ cup brown rice flour

½ cup chickpea flour

¼ cup dark buckwheat flour, plus more for rolling

½ teaspoon xanthan gum

½ teaspoon sea salt

6 tablespoons unsalted butter, cold and cut into cubes

2–4 tablespoons ice water

milk, for brushing

evaporated cane sugar or coconut sugar

For the Bumbleberry Filling

5 cups fresh or frozen mixed berries (I like a raspberry, blackberry, and blueberry mixture)

2 tablespoons honey

2 teaspoons balsamic vinegar

2 tablespoons water

2 teaspoons arrowroot flour

For Serving

vanilla ice cream

MAKE AHEAD

All-Butter Pastry: 2 days; 1 month, frozen (unbaked dough).

Bumbleberry Filling: 4 days.

Make the All-Butter Pastry: Preheat oven to 375°F. In a food processor, blend flours, xanthan gum, and salt. Add butter and pulse until a coarse meal. Add ice water, 1 tablespoon at a time, until dough holds together but is not wet.

Dust a clean counter and rolling pin with buckwheat flour; add dough (no chilling required), shape into a disk, and roll until ¼-inch thick, adding more flour as needed. Using a round cookie cutter or glass rim, cut rounds of dough (you'll get about 10 rounds) and place on a large-rimmed baking sheet, spacing 1 inch apart. Bake for 15–20 minutes, until dough is puffed and beginning to brown. Cool on baking sheet until ready to serve.

Make the Bumbleberry Filling: In a large pot, add berries, honey, and balsamic vinegar. Cook over medium-high heat until berries begin to let out juices. Reduce to a simmer, partially cover, and cook for 5 minutes. In a small bowl, combine water and arrowroot; stir into berries and cook, stirring constantly, for 1 minute longer, until glossy and thickened.

To Serve: To bowls, add a generous scoop (or two) of ice cream, spoon over berries, and top with a couple pastry rounds. Serve.

THE BIG BOWL OF COOKIE DOUGH

Yes, yes, I know the idea of beans in dessert is just plain weird, but you'll soon get over that fact at first bite. Play around with a chocolate brownie variation including black beans and cocoa powder, or skip the chocolate altogether for an oatmeal raisin alternative with rolled oats, cinnamon, and juicy raisins. Simple, kid-friendly, and crowd-pleasing.

Serves 6

For the Cookie Dough

2 cups cooked chickpeas or white navy beans (great northern beans)

⅓ cup coconut oil, melted and cooled slightly (as to not melt chocolate)

¼ cup maple syrup

2 teaspoons vanilla extract

½ teaspoon sea salt (omit if using canned beans with added salt)

3 tablespoons coconut flour

½ cup mini chocolate chips or 2–3 ounces dark chocolate, finely chopped

For Serving

apple slices

gluten-free graham crackers

Make the Cookie Dough: In a food processor, blend beans until smooth. Add oil, maple syrup, vanilla, and salt; blend again for 30 seconds–1 minute until creamy. Add coconut flour, blend, scrape sides, and blend again. Pulse in chocolate until just incorporated. Transfer dough to a large serving bowl, cover and chill for 2 hours.

To Serve: Present the bowl of cookie dough like you would hummus, with apple slices and gluten-free graham crackers for dipping. Alternatively, chill dough and roll into truffles.

MAKE AHEAD

Cookie Dough: 1 week.

SUNNY CITRUS BOWLS WITH ORANGE POMEGRANATE SALSA AND LEMON CREAM

This sparkly, jewel-toned salsa begs for something creamy—and that's exactly what it gets. An innocent-appearing, vanilla bean–speckled cream hides sharp lemon and a hint of coconut, cutting through a bit of the cream's richness (but not too much). It's this ethereal citrus cloud that makes the entire bowl feel dessert appropriate. You can make this year-round, but be sure to take advantage of peak citrus season during the winter—coincidentally prime time for pomegranates—when we could all use a little more sunshine in our lives.

.... *Serves 4* ....

For the Lemon Cream

1 cup 35% heavy whipping cream

2 tablespoons maple syrup

½ teaspoon vanilla bean paste or vanilla extract

¼ cup chilled coconut milk (thick, canned)

2 tablespoons lemon juice

For the Orange Pomegranate Salsa

3–4 mixed oranges (cara cara, blood oranges, clementine, etc.), peeled and sliced into a mixture of segments and rounds.

1 cup pomegranate seeds

To Serve

Unsweetened coconut flakes or unsweetened shredded coconut

> **MAKE AHEAD**
>
> *Lemon Cream:*
> 3 hours.
>
> *Orange Pomegranate Salsa:* 3 hours.

Make the Lemon Cream: In a stand mixer or with a hand mixer fitted with a whisk attachment, whip cream until soft peaks form. Add maple syrup, vanilla, and coconut milk; whip until firm peaks form. Add lemon juice and whip just to incorporate (do not over-whip). Cover and refrigerate until ready to serve.

Make the Orange Pomegranate Salsa: In a medium bowl, gently combine all salsa ingredients.

To Serve: To bowls, add salsa; dollop with cream and sprinkle with coconut. Serve.

DANISH RISALAMANDE WITH CARDAMOM CHERRIES

Having a Danish background gives me all sorts of authority over rice pudding, a traditional dessert served around the holidays in Scandinavia. Growing up, I've been told stories by my dad about his Danish grandmother's rice pudding containing a single, whole almond; the lucky diner that finds the whole almond in their bowl is said to have good luck in the new year. Customarily punctuated with cherry compote (it's not to be skipped, I'm told), I've done the same, with my version capitalizing on the florid notes of Scandinavia's trademark baking spice, cardamom. Don't wait for the holidays to make this Danish delicacy.

Serves 6

For the Risalamande

2 cups water

2 cups unsweetened plain almond milk or milk of choice

¾ cup white arborio rice (no substitutions)

½ teaspoon sea salt

3 tablespoons maple syrup

2 teaspoons vanilla extract or vanilla bean paste

1 teaspoon almond extract

1 cup 35% heavy whipping cream, whipped

½ cup whole blanched almonds, 1 whole blanched almond reserved, remaining chopped

Cardamom Cherries

2 cups frozen, unsweetened dark pitted cherries or fresh cherries, pitted

¼ cup unsweetened cherry juice or water

1 tablespoon maple syrup

½ teaspoon ground cardamom

¼ teaspoon ground cinnamon

pinch, sea salt

1 teaspoon lemon juice

> **MAKE AHEAD**
>
> *Risalamande:* 1 week.
>
> *Cardamom Cherries:* 1 week.

Make the Risalamande: In a large pot, bring water, milk, rice, and salt to a boil, stirring constantly. Reduce to medium/medium-low and cook, uncovered, for 35–45 minutes, stirring often (reduce heat to low nearing the end of cooking time to avoid splatters, if necessary). Remove from heat and stir in maple syrup and extracts. Cool to room temperature and refrigerate for at least 4 hours or overnight. After risalamande is chilled, gently fold in whipped cream, followed by chopped almonds and the 1 reserved whole almond. Chill until ready to eat.

Make the Cardamom Cherries: In a medium saucepan, bring cherries, juice or water, maple syrup, cardamom, cinnamon, and salt to a boil, reduce to a simmer, and cook, uncovered, for 10 minutes. Remove from heat and stir in lemon juice. Keep warm or chill.

To Serve: To bowls, add risalamande; drape over compote, being sure to include a balance of whole cherries and juice. Serve.

ROASTED PEARS WITH WHIPPED GOAT CHEESE AND MAPLE PINE NUT BRITTLE

Baked with a cinnamon stick, topped with a pillow of whipped goat cheese, and crowned with a shimmering maple syrup pine nut brittle, this dessert walks that delicate line between rustic and sophisticated. Here, the pears are their own bowls, allowing you to eat them by hand straight from the refrigerator, or, if you feel like being dainty, in a shallow (real) bowl with a spoon.

.... *Serves 4* ....

For the Roasted Pears

4 ripe bartlett or bosc pears, halved and cored

1 cinnamon stick, halved

For the Maple Pine Nut Brittle

¼ cup pine nuts

2 tablespoons maple syrup

¼ teaspoon sea salt

For the Whipped Goat Cheese

3 ounces fresh goat cheese, room temperature

⅓ cup 35% heavy whipping cream

2 teaspoons lemon juice

1 teaspoon vanilla bean paste or vanilla extract

MAKE AHEAD

Whipped Goat Cheese: 1 week.

Roasted Pears: 2 days.

Maple Pine Nut Brittle: 2 days.

Make the Roasted Pears: Preheat oven to 375°F. To a 9x13-inch ceramic baking dish, add pears, flesh side up, and cinnamon stick. Bake for 35 minutes, until tender. Leave oven on.

Make the Maple Pine Nut Brittle: On a large-rimmed baking sheet lined with parchment paper, toss pine nuts with maple syrup and salt; spread in an even layer and bake for 10 minutes. Nuts will crisp and turn into brittle as they cool.

Make the Whipped Goat Cheese: In a medium bowl, whisk goat cheese until smooth. Whisk in cream, lemon juice, and vanilla, beating until smooth. Chill until ready to use.

To Serve: Top each pear half with a dollop of whipped goat cheese and crumble over pine nuts. Serve warm or chilled.

MINT CHOCOLATE STRACCIATELLA GELATO

For me, nothing says summertime like a bowl of gelato. I consider myself an aficionado, having tried many around the world, including its birthplace, Italy, where we first fell in love. Try as I might, I still can't replicate my absolute favorite flavor, pistachio, at home, but I can come pretty close to the mint chip and stracciatella varieties. I opt for fresh mint instead of extract and skip the green dye. For the stracciatella (branching from the Italian term for "to tear" as it resembles ripped sheets or shreds), dark chocolate is melted with coconut oil for cocoa snowflakes that deliquesce ever so softly on your tongue.

Makes 2 pints

Mint Chocolate Stracciatella Gelato

2 cups 35% heavy whipping cream

1 ounce fresh mint leaves, stems included, plus more for serving

2 teaspoons vanilla extract

2 cups whole milk

⅓ cup evaporated cane sugar

¼ teaspoon sea salt

2 egg yolks

½ cup (3 ounces) dark chocolate chips

¼ cup coconut oil

Make the Mint Chocolate Stracciatella Gelato: In a medium saucepan, bring cream and mint leaves to a boil. Remove from heat, cover, and steep for 10 minutes. Using a mesh sieve, strain into a large bowl (one with a pouring spout is handy), pressing firmly down on mint leaves with the back of a spoon to extract maximum flavor. Stir in vanilla.

In a large high-sided skillet or large pot, bring milk, sugar, and salt to a gentle boil; reduce to medium-low and quickly stir to dissolve sugar. Add a ladle of hot milk to egg yolks to temper. Add yolks to hot milk and cook over medium-low, stirring often with a heatproof rubber scraper or wooden spoon for 5–10 minutes (be sure not to overheat or you'll scramble the eggs). Add to cream mixture, stir, cover tightly, and refrigerate for at least 8 hours (overnight best), until cold.

In a small saucepan over low heat, melt chocolate chips with coconut oil. Cool for 10 minutes (make sure it's still liquid).

Turn on ice cream maker. Pour in chilled cream mixture and freeze according to manufacturer's directions (generally 20–25 minutes for gelato). In last 2 minutes of churning, very slowly drizzle in melted chocolate mixture a little at a time, breaking up any large chunks that form with a spoon. Stop machine. Transfer immediately to an airtight container and freeze for at least 5 hours.

To Serve: Scoop into bowls and garnish with a few mint leaves. Serve.

MAKE AHEAD

Mint Chocolate Stracciatella Gelato: 1 week.

Chapter 5: Homemade Extras and Basics

Final flourishes and strong basics are the glue that hold these recipes together—they add character, texture, wow-factor, and often, increase the nutritional profile. A simple sauce or dressing can act as a nod to a country's cuisine, adding richness, depth, and sating power. While most of the bowls in this book have their sauces, dressings, and condiments on the same recipe page, this chapter includes the everyday extras that will feel at home in your kitchen (and in your bowl) any time of year. Furthermore, this section includes a guide to roasting nuts, making nut butter, pressing tofu, and a handy whole grain cooking chart. Employ any of these bonuses using **The Whole Bowls Formula** for something completely new and appealing to you.

HOMEMADE EXTRAS AND BASICS

BALSAMIC GLAZE

Balsamic glaze is the tuxedoed member of the vinegar family. Gorgeously eggplant-purple, jammy, and sweet. Drizzled over any bowl, savory or sweet, it adds a strikingly gourmet appearance and tang.

.... *Makes ¼ cup* ....

1 cup balsamic vinegar

In a small saucepan, bring vinegar to a boil (turn on your exhaust fan and stand back so you don't choke on the vinegar steam), reduce to medium, and cook for 15 minutes, until reduced to ¼ cup. Store in a glass jar in the pantry for up to 6 months.

QUICK HARISSA

This is a cheater's harissa using dried chili flakes and tomato paste. It's on the mild side, so heat seekers may want to add more spice.

2 cloves garlic
¼ cup extra-virgin olive oil
1 (5.5-ounce) can tomato paste
1 tablespoon lemon juice
1 tablespoon chili flakes
1 tablespoon smoked paprika
2 teaspoons caraway seeds
2 teaspoons ground cumin

In a food processor, pulse garlic until minced. Add remaining ingredients, blend, scrape sides, and blend again until smooth. Transfer to a glass jar or airtight container and store in refrigerator for up to 2 weeks. Or, freeze tablespoon-sized portions on a parchment lined baking sheet, transfer frozen portions to a zip-top bag, and freeze for up to 2 months; take out portions as needed, defrosting before use.

HOMEMADE MAYONNAISE

It's hard to go back to store-bought mayonnaise after trying this. For best results, be sure to source the freshest eggs possible.

Makes 1¼ cups

1 large egg
1 tablespoon lemon juice
1 teaspoon Dijon mustard

½ teaspoon honey
½ teaspoon sea salt
½ cup extra-virgin olive oil

½ cup neutral vegetable oil (refined avocado oil works well)

To a blender or food processor, add egg, lemon juice, mustard, honey, and salt. Blend until combined. With machine running, in a slow, steady stream, add oils through the chute. Blend just until thick (10–15 seconds once all oil is in; over-blending will break mayonnaise). Transfer to a glass jar or airtight container and store in refrigerator for up to 1 week.

APRICOT MUHAMMARA

Instead of the classic brick-red muhammara, this one is gorgeously canary colored. The sticky-smooth texture comes from syrupy, slightly sour dried apricots, lending a new base to the traditional Syrian recipe. It's a hearty paste that speaks to the bold, assertive flavors more of us are warming up to as weeknight staples.

1 yellow bell pepper, halved and seeded
1 clove garlic
1 cup dried apricots
⅓ cup white sesame seeds
1½ teaspoons ground cumin
1 teaspoon chili flakes, more to taste
½ teaspoon smoked or mild paprika
½ teaspoon sea salt
½ cup water
¼ cup extra-virgin olive oil
1 tablespoon lemon juice

Preheat oven to 400°F. Line a medium-rimmed baking sheet or square pan with parchment paper. Place pepper skin-side up on parchment. Roast for 30 minutes.

In a food processor, pulse garlic until minced. Add roasted pepper (leave skin intact), apricots, sesame seeds, spices, and salt; pulse again until minced. Add water, oil, and lemon; blend, scraping sides once or twice until a smooth paste forms. Store in an airtight container in the refrigerator for up to 3 weeks.

PUMPKIN SEED SAUCE

While the pastel green hue of this sauce is hushed, the flavor certainly isn't. Try it with Mexican flavors, as a salad dressing, drizzled over warm short-grain brown rice (how I love it), splash on roasted sweet potatoes, or as a dip for vegetables.

½ cup plus 2 tablespoons very hot, recently boiled water
⅓ cup pumpkin seeds
1 clove garlic, minced
2 tablespoons lime juice
1 tablespoon pumpkin seed oil or extra-virgin olive oil
1 tablespoon maple syrup
1 teaspoon ground cumin
1 teaspoon sea salt

Add all sauce ingredients to a blender and blend until smooth. Store in a glass jar or airtight container in refrigerator for up to 4 days; shake or stir before using.

TRADITIONAL HUMMUS

Many years ago, I dined at a hummus-only restaurant in New York City (the name escapes me) and was completely taken with their heavy-handed application of plush tahini, as well as big, swirling, golden glugs of olive oil on top—not within the recipe itself. However good that summer evening of feasting on hummus was (and it was very—earlier that night I locked eyes with Daniel Craig (James Bond) on the sidewalk, which really added to the event), the pinnacle of my many hummus experiences was at the celebrated Israeli restaurant, Shaya, in New Orleans.

The hummus at Shaya was served with wood-fired pita, which I could see being stretched and baked in my peripheral vision. And lucky me, the chef came out to talk to his patrons that evening, so naturally, I asked him what the secret to his nonpareil hummus was. He told me: taking the translucent outer skin off each and every chickpea. I seldom do this, but it's something you can try if you want to impress your friends (or yourself) and have a bit of spare time on your hands.

1–2 cloves garlic
2 cups cooked chickpeas, skinned if you want this extra creamy and have plenty of extra time
⅓ cup tahini
¼ cup lemon juice
¼ cup water, plus more to thin
2 teaspoons ground cumin
½ teaspoon sea salt
ground black pepper, to taste
extra-virgin olive oil, for serving

In a food processor, pulse garlic until finely chopped. Add remaining ingredients except oil, blend for 1 minute, scrape down sides, and blend again until creamy. If too thick for your liking, add water 1 tablespoon at a time until desired consistency. Check for seasoning, adding more salt if necessary. To serve, swirl into a shallow bowl, creating a "moat" with the back of a spoon; drizzle olive oil in the "moat." Cover and refrigerate leftovers for up to 1 week. Bring to room temperature before serving for best flavor and texture.

ROMESCO

A thick, brick-hued condiment that no kitchen repertoire should be without. Try it tossed with pasta, used as a dip for crostini, pita, or roasted mini new potatoes, spread on a sandwich, eaten by the spoonful—you get the idea.

1 red bell pepper, seeded and halved
⅓ cup roasted almonds
1 (5.5-ounce) can tomato paste
2 cloves garlic, peeled
¼ cup extra-virgin olive oil
3 tablespoons red wine vinegar
2 teaspoons mild smoked paprika
2 teaspoons sea salt

Preheat oven to 425°F. Line a medium-rimmed baking sheet with parchment paper. Place pepper skin-side up and roast for 25–30 minutes. In a food processor, pulse garlic until minced. Add roasted pepper, tomato paste, almonds, olive oil, vinegar, paprika, and salt. Blend until smooth. Store in an airtight container or glass jar in the refrigerator for up to 2 weeks, or freeze for up to 2 months.

COCONUT DREAMY WHIP

A plant-based substitution for whipped cream. This is just as delightful when used to garnish a more complex dessert as it is paired simply with a big bowl of berries for dipping. (For this, I like to stir in a little sour cream and have a bowl of brown sugar handy—no longer dairy-free, but a decadent seasonal treat I look forward to.)

1 (14-ounce) can full-fat coconut milk, chilled overnight, unshaken (do not use 'lite' as it will not whip correctly)
1–2 tablespoons maple syrup (optional)

Open can and carefully scoop out rich coconut cream into the bowl of a stand mixer fitted with a whisk attachment, or large bowl if whipping by hand with a balloon whisk. Reserve clear coconut water on bottom for another use (smoothies, curries, cooking rice, etc.). Whip on high until fluffy (about 2 minutes), or whip vigorously by hand until voluminous. Add maple syrup to taste (if using). Store in refrigerator for up to 1 day or use immediately.

HOMEMADE NUT BUTTER

With the amount of nut butter I go through, I'd be broke if I bought it. Beyond the economical perk of DIY nut butter, another feature of making it at home is coming up with your own proprietary blends (suggestions below).

2–4 cups roasted nuts or seeds (almonds, walnuts, hazelnuts, peanuts, pistachios, sunflower seeds, or a mixture) (see page **206**)

Add nuts or seeds (or a mixture) to a food processor and blend for 3–5 minutes, or until a ball forms. Break into pieces and blend again until oils release and they begin to get creamy (about 3–5 minutes). Turn off machine for 10 minutes (as to not overheat motor). Scrape sides and blend until completely smooth (about 3–5 minutes). Transfer to a glass jar or airtight container and refrigerate for up to 1 month. Stir before using.

NOTES

Raw nuts and seeds can be used in lieu of roasted, but the flavor will be toned down. Raw nuts and seeds also don't get as creamy, leaving you with a coarser, thicker texture.

Nut Butter Mix Suggestions

Use a 1:1 ratio for best results

Almond + Walnut

Almond + Hazelnut

Hazelnut + Peanut

Peanut + Sunflower seeds

Sunflower seeds + Pumpkin seeds

Walnut + Raw hulled hemp hearts

ROASTING NUTS AND SEEDS

Roasting nuts and seeds extracts the full-bodied, nutty notes locked within these miniscule baubles by coaxing out the delicate oils.

For the Roasted Nuts and Seeds

Raw nuts or seeds (amount as per recipe's instruction, or roast in bulk)

Preheat oven to 300°F. Add nuts or seeds to a large-rimmed baking sheet. Roast for specified time (see below). Nuts should be aromatic and uniformly tanned when cut in half; seeds should be aromatic, slightly puffed, and tanned on exterior. Cool before storing in an airtight container or zip-top bag in refrigerator for up to 6 months or freezer for up to 1 year.

Roasting Times

Almonds: 18–20 minutes

Hazelnuts: 18–20 minutes (once cool, place in a large pasta colander in the sink and move around until skin falls off)

Peanuts: 15–20 minutes

Pumpkin seeds: 10–15 minutes

Sunflower seeds: 10–15 minutes

Walnuts: 15–20 minutes

NOTES

Use only shelled (hulled) raw or shelled (hulled) blanched nuts and seeds.

All roasting times approximate. Keep an eye on them.

BOOSTER TOPPING

A hearty, textural finisher I created one Christmas Eve for the following morning's breakfast. Try the topping on hot oatmeal with maple syrup and bananas, or warm grains with tamari, sesame oil, and sliced scallions; add crunch factor to salads, curries, and soups; sprinkle on yogurt, ice cream, and rice pudding; or simply eat out of hand as trail mix. Reduce or increase the amounts according to your needs and experiment with the nuts and seeds you have handy.

1 cup walnuts, chopped
½ cup unsweetened coconut chips or flakes
⅓ cup pumpkin seeds

In a large skillet, add all ingredients. Toast over medium heat for 1–2 minutes, until fragrant. Transfer to a bowl to cool completely before storing in an airtight container or jar in the pantry for up to 2 months.

PRESSING TOFU

Pressing transforms the texture of the tofu into something much heartier, meatier, and available to soak up whatever flavors you throw at it. Even extra-firm tofu benefits from removing additional water, of which there is a surprising amount. Pressing can turn you from a tofu avoider into a tofu hoarder.

Tofu presses are available but they're uncommon in most kitchens, so I've provided my (unconventional and sometimes precarious) method for pressing without a true press.

1. Begin with a package of extra-firm tofu. Drain water from package and place on a large plate.

2. Place a baking sheet or large cast-iron skillet over tofu. Stack a ceramic coated cast-iron pot or a few heavy books on top (nudging them against the wall is helpful to avoid it toppling over).

3. Keep pressed for 2 hours or longer. Discard water on plate. Prepare as per recipe instructions.

WHOLE GRAIN COOKING CHART

Grains: 1 cup dry	Liquid	Cooking Time	Directions	Yield	Notes
Amaranth	3 cups	20	Bring grain and water to a boil; simmer, cover, and cook for directed time.	3 cups	Cooks into a thick, creamy porridge.
Buckwheat groats and Kasha	1¾ cups	12	Bring grain and water to a boil; simmer, cover, and cook for directed time.	3 cups	Be careful not to overcook.
Grits, white, creamy old fashioned	3–4 cups	20	Bring grain and water to a boil; simmer, cover, and cook, whisking often, for directed time.	2½ cups	Can be used instead of polenta.
Millet	2 cups	20	Bring grain and water to a boil; simmer, cover, and cook for directed time. Steam for 5 minutes; fluff with fork.	3 cups	Use as a gluten-free couscous alternative.
Oats, steel cut	4 cups	20–25	Bring grain and water to a boil, reduce to medium-low, and cook uncovered, stirring often, for directed time.	4 cups	Salt is needed to bring out the flavor.
Quinoa	2 cups	15	Bring grain and water to a boil; simmer, cover, and cook for directed time. Steam for 5 minutes; fluff with fork.	3 cups	Try white, black, and red varieties.
Rice, black	2 cups	45	Bring grain and water to a boil; simmer, cover, and cook for directed time. Steam for 5 minutes; fluff with fork.	3 cups	Rich in antioxidants and full of flavor.
Rice, brown basmati	1¾ cups	45	Bring grain and water to a boil; simmer, cover, and cook for directed time. Steam for 5 minutes; fluff with fork.	3 cups	Use to make fragrant pilafs or employ as a bed for curries.
Rice, short grain brown	2 cups	45	Bring grain and water to a boil; simmer, cover, and cook for directed time. Steam for 5 minutes; fluff with fork.	3 cups	My favorite grain and the most versatile.
Rice, wild	3 cups	45	Bring grain and water to a boil; simmer, cover, and cook for directed time. Drain excess water.	3 cups	Excellent for both warm and cold salads.

Acknowledgments

A great deal of thanks is due to many people.

To my literary agent, Carly Watters, who believed in this cookbook from the moment we started talking. Her knowledge, endurance, and publishing world savvy have been indispensible. Carly's guidance and well-timed advice has helped me grow as both an author and businessperson.

To my editor at Skyhorse Publishing in New York, Nicole Frail, who has been on-call to answer all of my first-time author dilemmas—of which there have been many. The passion she has for her job, seeing books come from blank pages with blinking cursors to hardbacks, captivated me throughout the entire process.

Of course, thank you to the readers of my blog, *Yummy Beet*, and everyone I've connected with over social media, email, and in person because of the words I write, food I cook, and photos I take each week. It brings me incomparable pleasure to see people get excited about vegetables and plant-based cuisine. Appreciation also to the blogging friends I've made in both real life and online (and online, then in real life), who continually put themselves out there sharing kitchen creations, personal stories, and food as art. I love my blogging community with all of my heart.

Thank you to Martha Stewart, whom I've never met, but who propelled me into the kitchen in the first place so I had to include her (plus, I just really wanted to write that). Martha Stewart has been my female food entrepreneurial idol since I was eleven years old and I'm probably going to move my cookbook next to her many in the bookstore when no one is looking.

And thank you most of all to my family who have supported me with their kind words, smiles, recipe feedback, and extraordinary patience.

Thank you to my sister, Kirsten: smoothie and sweet potato fry guru, the most brutally honest taste tester in town. When I don't have time to dance around deciding if a recipe tastes "cookbook worthy" or not, she's who I call. While Kirsten doesn't do the dishes, she makes me laugh like no one else can (away, beast). For my brother, Stewart: eggy sandwich master; sister-in-law, Katie: baker and entertainer extraordinaire; and their children, who make my life infinitely more fun, balanced, and let's be honest, cute (thanks to their kids, that is—but Stew and Katie are actually pretty cute, too).

Finally, my dad, my best bud, Kimball: king of pasta puttanesca. I was overjoyed to share each and every recipe with him, even though he thought everything was a "winner" (when it was clearly no such thing). Like my beloved bowls, I know he's within reach whenever I'm in need.

Index

Conversion Charts

METRIC AND IMPERIAL CONVERSIONS

(These conversions are rounded for convenience)

Ingredient	Cups/Tablespoons/Teaspoons	Ounces	Grams/Milliliters
Butter	1 cup=16 tablespoons= 2 sticks	8 ounces	230 grams
Cream cheese	1 tablespoon	0.5 ounce	14.5 grams
Cheese, shredded	1 cup	4 ounces	110 grams
Cornstarch	1 tablespoon	0.3 ounce	8 grams
Flour, all-purpose	1 cup/1 tablespoon	4.5 ounces/0.3 ounce	125 grams/8 grams
Flour, whole wheat	1 cup	4 ounces	120 grams
Fruit, dried	1 cup	4 ounces	120 grams
Fruits or veggies, chopped	1 cup	5 to 7 ounces	145 to 200 grams
Fruits or veggies, puréed	1 cup	8.5 ounces	245 grams
Honey, maple syrup, or corn syrup	1 tablespoon	.75 ounce	20 grams
Liquids: cream, milk, water, or juice	1 cup	8 fluid ounces	240 milliliters
Oats	1 cup	5.5 ounces	150 grams
Salt	1 teaspoon	0.2 ounces	6 grams
Spices: cinnamon, cloves, ginger, or nutmeg (ground)	1 teaspoon	0.2 ounce	5 milliliters
Sugar, brown, firmly packed	1 cup	7 ounces	200 grams
Sugar, white	1 cup/1 tablespoon	7 ounces/0.5 ounce	200 grams/12.5 grams
Vanilla extract	1 teaspoon	0.2 ounce	4 grams